MW01484829

WHY
NO ONE
IS BUYING
YOUR
PRODUCT

WHY NO ONE IS BUYING YOUR PRODUCT

9 STEPS TO CREATE PRODUCTS AND SERVICES THAT CUSTOMERS LOVE, SELL MORE, AND INCREASE PROFITS.

SHERWETTE

Why No One Is Buying Your Product
© Copyright 2022 Sherwette Mansour

All rights reserved. No part of this publication may be reproduced, distributed, or transmitted in any form or by any means, including photocopying, recording, or other electronic or mechanical methods, without the prior written permission of the publisher, except in the case of brief quotations embodied in critical reviews and certain other noncommercial uses permitted by copyright law.

Although the author and publisher have made every effort to ensure that the information in this book was correct at press time, the author and publisher do not assume and hereby disclaim any liability to any party for any loss, damage, or disruption caused by errors or omissions, whether such errors or omissions result from negligence, accident, or any other cause.

Adherence to all applicable laws and regulations, including international, federal, state, and local governing professional licensing, business practices, advertising, and all other aspects of doing business in the US, Canada, or any other jurisdiction, is the sole responsibility of the reader and consumer.

Neither the author nor the publisher assumes any responsibility or liability whatsoever on behalf of the consumer or reader of this material. Any perceived slight of any individual or organization is purely unintentional.

For more information, email me@sherwette.com
ISBN: 978-9948-19-413-2

PRAISE FOR WHY NO ONE IS BUYING YOUR PRODUCT

"Do you want engaged customers who eagerly await the opportunity to do business with you? Better yet, do you want your customers to send their family and friends your way? In Why No One is Buying Your Product, Sherwette Mansour brilliantly provides straightforward, practical, and memorable tools for ensuring repeat and referral business. This book is for anyone who wants to create a customer-centric culture that produces meteoric business and personal success. Run to the counter or click 'buy now' to access this transformative, refreshing, and much-needed resource."

Joseph Michelli, Ph.D. Certified Customer Experience Consultant, New York Times #1 bestselling author of books like *Stronger Through Adversity*, *The New Gold Standard*, and *The Starbucks Experience*.

YOUR FREE QUIZ!

"What's Your Product Design Personality?"

Before reading any further, I would love to invite you to take the quiz, **"What's Your Product Design Personality?"**

I have created this assessment specifically to help you identify your personality and preferences when designing new products or services. You see, based on your strengths, you may choose to do certain activities over others. One of the top mistakes I see repeatedly is innovators creating products or services without following a proven process, or perhaps, "forgetting" some of the crucial steps, which leads to creating products that no one buys.

If I am being honest, I too fell into that very same trap and had been stalling for years, "skipping" some steps even though I knew exactly what I needed to do. What I have realized is that sometimes we get in our own way. Even though we might know what needs to be done, because we don't necessarily want to do it, we stop ourselves. This led me to create this assessment.

By knowing your *Product Design Personality*, you will know your strengths and fill in the gaps by ensuring that you or your team do the activities you might have otherwise overlooked and create a bulletproof product or service.

To get the best experience from this book, I've found that readers who take the quiz **"What's Your Product Design Personality?"** can implement these proven methods faster and continue following the required steps to create products or services that customers love and sell more of them, thus increasing profits.

You can take the free quiz by visiting:

https://www.sherwette.com/quiz

This book is dedicated to my mother, who has forever believed in me and supported me with everything she has.

FOREWORD

Most new products don't survive. Only one in twenty succeed.
What about the other nineteen? Nobody expected them to fail
– not the teams that created them, nor the teams that marketed
them. These products were supposed to meet customer needs
better than current products. They were based on customer
research and designed by smart people. So, how did so many of
them end up in the graveyard of failed product launches?

A few of these failures can be attributed to unexpected changes in
the marketplace. This century is still young, but we've already seen
a global financial crisis and a global pandemic. Products that were
certain to succeed before these events occurred were suddenly
failures because customer needs and circumstances changed
overnight.

Most product failures, however, are due not to dramatic
external changes but to the innovators and marketers who didn't

understand their customers. They thought they did, but ultimately the marketplace proved otherwise. My own experience with new products that failed to meet expectations bears this out. We always thought we were meeting a pressing customer need but later inevitably found that we didn't really understand the customer's true situation and motivation.

I first encountered Sherwette through her writing about consumer behavior. Her engaging style and keen insight led me to invite her to contribute to my blog, *Neuromarketing*. I'm happy and proud to see Sherwette take her writing and ideas to the next level.

Sherwette's passion for understanding and serving the customer shines through in her writing. She likes to see happy customers.

Why No One Is Buying Your Product is Sherwette's contribution to those who are on the journey of creating products and services. Her writing style is just like her blog: easy, bite-sized, and digestible. This practical guide will help you create products and services that buck the odds and succeed in the marketplace.

It's truly a joy to create products and services that customers love, and this book will support you in your innovation journey.

Roger Dooley, Author of *Friction and Brainfluence*

TABLE OF
CONTENTS

How would you feel if you turned your product situation around, creating the value you always wanted, and your sales started to grow?

LETTER
TO THE
READER

Dear Reader,

I bet you grabbed this book because you are a bit like me. You want to hone your craft to create products and services that your customers will fall in love with again and again. You want to make an impact and provide value to your customers.

Or shall we state the obvious? Perhaps, maybe, no one is buying your product. I mean, really, what use would it be to spend hours developing your product, only to find out that you have no customers clicking "Add to Cart?"

1

Whether you are:
- Creating a new product or improving an existing one
- Just starting out or well established
- Well financed or barely scraping by

... you want reassurance that you are on the right path. Otherwise, you'd be spending all your time and money building products that no one needs or wants.

Perhaps it was you who came up with the brilliant idea, or it could have been your client who did, and you have put all your sweat, time, and effort to bring it to life, only to find your customer rejecting that unique solution of yours.

Sometimes ideas sound great in our heads ... But, in the end, are they profitable?

As Paul Graham said: *"Most startups fail because they are trying to fix a problem that doesn't exist."*

To get past this, you want to be very clear in your head about first, who you are trying to serve; second, what problem you are helping them with; third, if your solution is really working; and finally, if your customers even know about it. Once you get that clarity, you will repeatedly create products and services your customers love and use consistently—not to mention advocate for and recommend to others.

You want, and need, your customers to have more skin in the game.

Did you know?

Studies show that products and companies that do not innovate face the risk of failure. According to HBS professor Clayton Christensen,[1] 95% of all product innovations fail,[2] and according to the Startup Genome report,[3] 92% of startups fail.[4] In other words, 11 out of 12 startups fail, and 19 out of 20 product innovations fail. According to these numbers, that's a lot of failures.

The lack of following a product innovation process contributes to that failure.

In fact, most organizations, 82% to be exact, run innovation the same way they run regular operations according to an Accenture survey.[5] This results in a few challenges of its own, such as missing out on opportunities and being blindsided by their very own past mistakes, unable to learn from them.

Thankfully, you can take some practical and achievable steps to avoid these outcomes and create innovative products and services that your customers will want to buy, use, and recommend to others.

Now, I have been on both sides, helping clients create products and services, and—well, like you—I am also a customer! You see, I have always been customer-obsessed, but my passion deepened after having worked in the customer and digital domain. I can't help but see how each product or service can be better. It became part of my DNA, and the thing I love more than anything is to see customers happy with their buying decisions. I hate to see a customer who is unhappy or disappointed with a product or, worse, has a problem or need and is struggling to find a solution for it.

After all, every single one of us is a customer, including you. Yes, you. You earned your money the hard way, and you want to enjoy spending it. You want to be comfortable.

But haven't you noticed that when your income increases, so do your expenses?

You love to spend money, and so do your customers.

Why do you suppose that is?

We like to shop. We want to spend our hard-earned money because it makes us feel accomplished.

"We deserve nice things," we tell ourselves. We are special. And, we love to treat our loved ones to nice things because they are special, too.

So, if that's the case, you might be thinking, *"Then why is no one buying my product?"*

Hold your horses. I am getting to it.

My journey in consumer behavior research started over ten years ago when I realized it was quickly becoming one of my passions. If you are a multi-passionate person like me, you understand how hard it is to pick a passion and stick with it.

Nevertheless, I committed myself to learning everything I could on the subject, and it was never enough. So, I continued to crave more knowledge, and one day I realized I just *had* to share it with others.

Being multi-passionate is both a blessing and a curse, a trait that traces back to when I was 17 years old trying to choose my major for college. I was in love with almost every subject in school. I even loved typing class, and I am so grateful for it because it's a skill that I am proud to have mastered. Oh, I forgot to mention that I was the classic, typical "nerd." You know the type: the straight-A student most classmates don't like because they ruin the curve. This experience led me to the challenges of being a perfectionist. But that is the subject of another book.

Being good at everything in school was a challenge of its own. I know, "*What kind of problem is that?*" you might be thinking, right? Well, I had to choose the path I should take for college, or my "life," for that matter. At least, that's what I thought at the time.

I loved Chemistry and playing in the lab. So, I decided to take Pharmacy and Biotechnology, but it didn't take me more than five seconds to realize I didn't enjoy dissecting things. So, long story short, I switched majors. Then, I was awarded an unexpected scholarship to study Software Engineering in Malaysia. And I thought, *why not?* Who wouldn't want to explore Malaysia? In case you are wondering, it's gorgeous. I absolutely loved it.

So, I went for it and studied Software Engineering. Just as I enjoyed most subjects in school, I had similar circumstances in college, but

I enjoyed Programming and Human-Computer Interaction classes the most.

The reason why might surprise you.

Programming is logical, and that's what I love the most about it. You don't have to remember anything. You don't have to read much, memorize anything, or understand different people's theories in history. All you have to do is think logically and everything else falls into place. It's simple, straightforward code.

Human-Computer Interaction touched on human psychology and how both hardware and software design impacts how we, as users, interact with it. During this course, I had an "aha" moment when I learned about the design of ATMs.

Think about this.

Every time you want to do something, there are multiple preliminary tasks that must be performed to get the job done.

Have you noticed that every time you withdraw money from the ATM, you first have to grab your debit card out of the machine, and THEN your cash is disbursed by the ATM?

It's because you, as a user, go to the ATM with one "job" in mind. You want that cash in your wallet, and so once that job is done, you leave and forget about everything else. That's why you always have to grab your card out of the machine first and then the machine allows you to have your money second. Otherwise, you will forget your card after you get your cash because you're focused on the one job you had in mind. ATM designers know this and want the customer's experience when withdrawing money to run smoothly and efficiently. That's why you always grab your debit card first, and then you take the cash.

You see, understanding *why* intrigues my curiosity. It always fascinates me to understand what makes us buy, what makes us behave in specific ways, and why we choose some brands over others.

Having a background in structured programming and software engineering taught me how to apply logic to everything. Coupled with my exquisite interest and research in understanding human behavior, I usually find a way to make a structure out of something that doesn't seem repeatable, then replicate it so others can easily follow the same process.

Once during a college study group, I used the metaphor of a two-piece bikini to teach my friends the concept of functions in object-oriented programming. When writing a function, you need to define it at the top, then write it. Two pieces of a function go hand in hand. Just like having a bikini, you want both pieces together. Otherwise, it's not really a bikini.

In this book, you'll find that I have fun ways to simplify and explain complex concepts, just like in the bikini example above.

Some people think product design and innovation result from some "creative muse," but in reality, they don't.

For over ten years, I have been researching, practicing, and deliberately learning about one of my favorite subjects, *Consumer Behavior and Psychology*. I have also chosen to change careers to management consulting in customer experience advisory because it gives me further real-life exposure to the subject where I can apply world-class methodologies and see the real impact it has on customers. I always tell people I practically have my dream job. That's not something many can say about their jobs.

Because of this and my passion for both my clients and customers, I wanted to share my knowledge with you. For a long time, I have been thinking about using this knowledge to serve others, saving them from doing all the same research and reading as many books or articles as I did. What if they can't afford the time and effort it takes to try and collect all the pieces together as I did?

And so, I have decided to write this book for you.
- Entrepreneurs
- Product managers
- Product designers
- Service designers
- Customer experience professionals
- Customer service managers
- Consultants
- Marketers
- Copywriters
- Anyone who wants to hone their skills to understand their market and competition

If that's you, then this book is for you. If you truly want to craft a product or service your customers will be raving about, then this book will help you gain a better understanding of your customers and create products that will be so spot-on that once they know about it, they will scream, "Here, take my money!"

It's probably tough for me to put together all that I have learned into one book, so instead, what I have aimed to do is share the best methodologies I have found and worked with. Some might have unique perspectives that will make you open your mind to different ways of thinking.

The methodologies in this book are not new. I did not invent them. However, I have simplified them based on my experience so that they will all make sense to you.

When I first started, I had no clue where to start, and each time I had an intellectual conversation with one of my colleagues or read a new book, I would have a new "aha" moment. It took me a long time to put all the puzzle pieces together, so I wanted to put them all together in one place, here in this book, so that you don't have to go through the same journey I did. Now start: right here.

Even if some of the concepts in this book aren't new to you, I encourage you to ask yourself what you can learn. It's human nature to know a lot of methods that we are too lazy to apply. However, when *using* these proven methods, I still get even more "aha" moments. So, bear with yourself, and trust the process.

There is no formula for creativity, but there is a process that will ignite your light, and this is what I intend to share with you in this book.

I have always been told that I am a creative person by whomever I've worked with, so I've wondered, *Is this a gift? Is this just who I am? What happens if someone wants to be creative but is not sure how to go about it?*

The answer is: we are all creative in our own way. Ideas don't just happen, but they can be seeded, and as you water them and follow through with the process, you will be rewarded with their fruition. And before you know it, you will be bombarded with so many ideas, you won't know where to begin.

> "In a field in which the rules are constantly changing-where the forces that determine the outcome are constantly shifting-where new problems are constantly being encountered every day-rules, formulas, and principles simply will not work. They are too rigid-too tightly bound to the past. They must be replaced by the only known method of dealing with the Constantly New-analysis."
> -Eugene Schwartz, Breakthrough Advertising[6]

You have picked up this book because you want to understand why no one is buying your product. You have put in the time and effort, but you are not getting the results you were hoping for.

Upon reading this simple guide, you will understand your market in ways you might not have ever even thought about before. You'll be able to create products and services that are innovative, provide great value to your customers, and increase your profits.

It starts with understanding your market, then creating your product, and then communicating that product back to your market. Each of the chapters in this book will, in detail, provide you with the understanding, tools, methodologies, and exercises that will help you "diagnose" your product. Note that each method is targeted for products or services; both words are interchangeable throughout this guide. And you will be able to go through each of the activities yourself and identify the "gap," or what could have gone wrong for you in the past.

Once you've applied all the methods you'll learn in this book, you will have your customers' skin in the game. They will be in it with you, and you will no longer be lost, alone in your own thoughts, thinking, *"What did I do wrong?"*

Not only that, but you will be in sync with everyone you collaborate with in the process to develop, market, and sell your product— including everyone you work with.

That will be awesome. Won't it?

Throughout this book, I will take you on your own personal journey so we can walk together to figure out exactly why no one is buying your product. Every chapter will focus on each step of the product innovation process to help you uncover those gaps that keep your customers from buying your product.

We will answer the following pressing questions:

- Who are your customers?
- What are your customers' challenges?
- What do they want to do better and faster in their lives?
- What are the desires that drive their actions?
- How do you craft a product that speaks to your customers and matches their desires?
- What do your customers experience when they interact with your product?
- ... and much, much more!

Ready to create products and services your customers love and grow your business?

With lots of love—
Your consumer behavior gal, ☺

−Sherwette

References

1. Carmen Nobel. "Clay Christensen's Milkshake Marketing." HBS Working Knowledge, February 14, 2011. https://hbswk.hbs.edu/item/clay-christensens-milkshake-marketing.

2. Startup Genome. "Reports." Startup Genome. Accessed September 17, 2021. https://startupgenome.com/report2017/.

3. Jesse Sumrak. "Failed Founders Reveal #1 Cause of Startup Death." Lendio, March 21, 2018. https://www.lendio.com/news/management-leadership/startup-death/.

4. Jesse Nieminen. "50+ Statistics on Innovation – What Do the Numbers Tell Us?" Viima. Viima Solutions Oy, October 10, 2018. https://www.viima.com/blog/innovation-stats.

5. Charles Hartley, and Anthony Suarez. "Three Years Later, U.S. Companies Continue to Struggle with Innovation, Accenture Survey Reveals." Newsroom. Accenture, March 21, 2016. https://newsroom.accenture.com/news/three-years-later-us-companies-continue-to-struggle-with-innovation-accenture-survey-reveals.htm.

6. Eugene Schwartz, and Edelston, Martin. "Breakthrough Advertising ." Breakthrough Advertising. Brian Kurtz, 2017. https://breakthroughadvertisingbook.com/.

HOW
THIS BOOK
WORKS

Whether it's products, services, or both, when applying the steps outlined in this book, the two terms are interchangeable, and these methodologies can be used in either situation. The best way to read this book is to go through all the chapters. Only then will you really understand all the different pieces of the puzzle to figure out what went wrong. At the end of each chapter, I've included exercises to help you put each theory into practice and really have an "aha moment" about your product.

But if you know where you stand in your business or product in some areas or have done these exercises before, you may choose to skip some chapters and go straight to the ones you feel will help you in your current situation. Then, you can go back and revisit any of the chapters at any point. You can continue using this book as a reference in the years to come, as innovation is a continuous process. You will find yourself going through these exercises again and again as you create new products or improve existing ones.

Innovation is not a linear process. A step further down the line may take you back to the drawing board again. It's a continuous process that you can follow even after achieving success because your customers' needs are constantly changing.

If you want to be on top of your game, understanding your customer is just the first step. Each chapter of this book focuses on a question that you must be able to answer about your customer and teaches you exactly how to answer it.

1. **Chapter 1:** *Who do you want to serve?* - Identifying and truly understanding your customer.
2. **Chapter 2:** *What do they want to do?* - Getting clear on the "jobs" your customer wants to do better and faster.
3. **Chapter 3:** *Why do they want to do it?* - Figuring out the desires that drive your customer's actions.
4. **Chapter 4:** *What is stopping them?* - Understanding your customer's challenges and pain points.
5. **Chapter 5:** *What problem are you helping them solve?* - Honing your products or services value proposition.
6. **Chapter 6:** *How does your product compare to other products on the market?* - Understanding where you stand compared to your competition in terms of price and quality.
7. **Chapter 7:** *How are you going to help them?* - Designing your customer experience to build lasting relationships.

8. **Chapter 8:** *Are you really helping them?* - Testing your products and services to see if there is market demand and whether they actually work.

9. **Chapter 9:** *Do they know about it?* - Crafting your message to match your customer's desires, awareness, and sophistication.

Oh, and one more thing: In this book, I use some of my favorite brands as examples to give some life to the methodologies. As I live in Dubai, I refer to brands local to the Middle East.

Shall we get started?

CHAPTER 1

Who Do You Want to Serve?

"If you try to please everyone, you'll please no one."
- Ricky Gervais

Chapter Objectives:

- **Personas**: Who is your customer?
- **Customer Research**: How do you populate the persona card?
- **Research Sample Size**: How much research is enough?
- **Research Approach Selection**: Which research method should you choose?

Getting your customers to buy your product should start with one thing, and one thing only—understanding your customers. That means understanding your customers so well that you understand them better than they understand themselves so you know exactly what is crossing their minds before they even open their mouths.

Like all great marketers, Ryan Levesque, the author of *Ask*, emphasizes knowing your market before you even think about creating your product. In fact, the reason I became hooked on the book *Ask*, eventually joined Ryan Levesque's program, and became his mentee was because Ryan clearly understood this concept.

I signed up for his email list upon reading the book. And although I do sign up for the email lists of many of today's marketing gurus, Ryan's list was different.

At the time that I signed up, Ryan was sending out a targeted campaign to learn more about his method, the Ask Method. At first, I thought, *Nah, I don't need it. I read the book. I can learn to apply the method on my own. After all, I am a management consultant in the Big 4, and I already know how to do all this stuff.*

This is my bread and butter!

But with every email I received, I felt like he was talking directly to me, just me. He was talking to Sherwette, not the masses. He was speaking to my desires, my fears, my challenges. He wanted to help me, and only me. First, I ignored it, but reading one email after the other, I was hooked. Finally, I bought into it, joined his program, and he became my mentor.

Sherwette Mansour
July 26, 2019 · 🌐   • • •

Guys, can I just say that Ryan Levesque is a marketing genius? I had zero intention on joining the class and thought I would just try to figure it out on my own after reading the book, but man, after reading every email he sends, every video he speaks in, every landing page that just says whatever I was thinking of, I can just say hands down, this guy is a mind reader. I can see myself being funneled in every thought... and that to be honest, is the reason I believe in the Ask method and I am excited to learn about it.

👍❤️ 41   45 Comments Seen by 5

He researched his customers so well, he was not only able to create a product that they would love to buy but also communicate it in such a way that made his target customers yell, *"Here, take my money!"*

Source- ComedyCentral

Do you know who you want to serve?

Every good entrepreneur, product designer, and marketer knows that pleasing everyone is an impossible task. The same goes for serving them.

If you decide to serve everyone, you may end up serving no one.

Keeping your market and your customers in mind is crucial when developing your product. You want to appeal to your customers in the same way I ended up on Ryan Levesque's mailing list and couldn't resist buying a few of his products. Understanding who you want to serve will help you design a product that caters to their needs and then identify marketing messages that appeal to that person.

Our natural instinct when designing a new product is to be generous and ambitious. We want to serve everyone. We want to touch the lives of as many people as we can.

But ... Should we?

The short answer is no, we shouldn't, and you shouldn't.

Things work differently when it comes to human behavior. We, as consumers, love to feel special. Of course, we want to know that we are unique, but more importantly, we have *specific needs, desires, and challenges* we want to have addressed.

One specific need I personally have as a curly-haired brunette is finding shampoo that will make my hair feel soft. The desire to have this need met means I am always on the lookout for the best shampoo that will meet this need. After all, like many women (and men), I want to feel beautiful. Between the two of us, that's my real desire. So, if I read a shampoo's product description that caters specifically to my curly hair type and color, I would say, *"Hey! Yes, that's me! Let me give it a try."* On the other hand, if I see a generic "silky smooth" advertisement for a mainstream 2-in-1 shampoo with no particular hair type in mind, I don't bother for a second; I already know it's not for me.

Now, let's take a look at the four components of understanding your customers' needs that we will be discussing in detail throughout this book.

1. **Desires** - What do your customers desire? *(More on that in Chapter 3: Why Do They Want to Do It?)*
2. **Awareness** - Do they know about that specific desire? *(More on that in Chapter 9: Do They Know about It?)*
3. **Challenges** – What is stopping them from fulfilling that desire? *(More on that in Chapter 4: What Is Stopping Them?)*
4. **Market Sophistication** - How much have they been looking to fulfill those desires, and what did they try before? *(More on that in Chapter 9: Do They Know about It?)*

The Four Components of Understanding Customers' Needs

Using the curly hair shampoo example, let's look at the four components of understanding your customers' needs.

1. **Desire:**
   - **Question:** What does your customer desire?
   - **Answer:** To look attractive. I have the desire to look beautiful.

2. **Awareness:**
   - **Question:** Do they know about that specific desire?
   - **Answer:** My awareness about that specific topic is very high, as with most people. (Of course, that's just one piece of the puzzle.)

3. **Challenges:**
   - **Question:** What is stopping them from fulfilling that desire?
   - **Answer:** No matter what vitamins I take, how many treatment creams I put on my hair, or expensive shampoos I buy, my hair's growth rate is so slow. And, by the time it grows out, I have to cut it because—guess what? Now I have split ends.

4. **Market sophistication:**
   - **Question:** How much have they been looking to fulfill those desires, and what did they try before?
   - **Answer:** Somewhat fulfilled desire; I've tried some products that I like, but they don't necessarily give me the ultimate look that I want.

Did you see what we just did here?

Understanding your customers, their desires, awareness levels, challenges, and market sophistication levels will help you figure out how you can help them.

TIP

How to spot market sophistication

Think, as a customer, I have a desire, and I am fully aware of it, but is my desire fulfilled?

Unfulfilled Desire:

Example: If I tried all Earthly products for my hair, both affordable and expensive, and I am still not happy with the results, I am not fulfilled.

Somewhat Fulfilled Desire:

Example: If I tried some products which I like, but don't necessarily give me the ultimate look that I want, then my desire is somewhat fulfilled.

Fulfilled Desire:

Example: If I look in the mirror in the morning, after my shower, or at any moment and I am happy with my hair, then my desire is fulfilled.

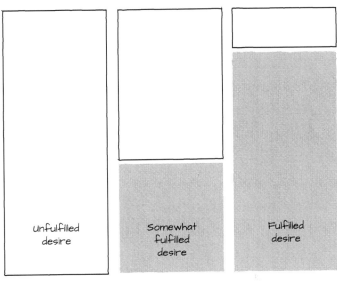

 DESIRE

Desire Fulfillment

Personas: *Who is your customer?*

Let me ask you a question ...

When you were in the creative process of developing this new product or service, what kind of person did you have in mind? Who are the one, two, or three people who inspired you?

These are the people who have practically driven your creative process. It's because of them you have put all your energy into designing and creating your product or service.

You might have someone in mind. How would you describe that someone? It's best to be as specific as possible, and I'll show you why.

Exhibit A: Women living in Dubai between the ages of 25 and 40.

Exhibit B: Sally is a 30-year-old workaholic. She is the creative director of an advertising agency with minimal time to get ready in the morning but must look absolutely stunning because her client-facing job depends on her image. She wants to look professional yet feminine. More importantly, she wants to feel like herself. Sally barely has any time for herself, so she tries to optimize how she spends it. She buys everything online, even groceries. She doesn't have enough time to cook but still tries to stay fit and healthy. She needs enough energy to keep her powering through the day. Sally enjoys going out for social gatherings to connect and network with other people, but she is practically glued to her devices. That's not to say she neglects personal relationships; on the contrary, she wants to devote every free moment to her fiancé. Above all, she wants to be the most beautiful woman in his eyes.

Women from the ages of 25 to 40 living in Dubai is a wide range. If you choose to target these metrics in Google Ads or Facebook Ads, your number of reaches will be huge. But does that mean you will convert that vast reach? If you think so, think again. At the heart of conversion is not the numbers—it's the heart.

Conversion happens when you touch the hearts and souls of your customers. Yes, you can target your chosen segment, but it doesn't mean that they will click on your ad once they see it. If they don't relate and "see themselves" in it, they won't bother. *(More on that in Chapter 9: Do They Know about It?)*

If you want to touch Sally's heart, you need to communicate with her in a language she understands. You have to dig deeper. You want to understand her desires and motivations, what she likes and dislikes, and what makes her tick. What is she trying to accomplish? What is stopping her?

You have to find out if she even knows she needs what you're offering. What else has she tried? Did it work for her, or is she on the edge of giving up?

Sounds great, but where to start? It seems like there is a lot to find out about Sally!

It starts with creating a persona.

> **A persona:** In the design world, a persona is a fictional character representing the customer using your product or service. It helps you identify their needs, experiences, behaviors, and goals.

I prefer my persona to be an actual, specific person. To me, it should be someone I can imagine myself talking to.

For each of the personas or characters you will be targeting, you want to know everything about them, or at the very least, as much as you can.

Think about it. If you can solve a problem for just one person, you will solve the same problem for all the other people who face that same problem. It's not the whole world, that's for sure, but it's going to touch the hearts and minds of the specific target segment that your persona represents. And, as Ricky Gervais said. *If you try to please everyone, you'll please no one.*

Now, let's talk about personas—I love personas. They are my favorite part of any new project. I get to learn about them and connect with them on an emotional level. They become part of my life.

Below is a list including all the information you want to know about the persona of your choice. Of course, one of the best ways for you to get this information is through social media. Or, shall we say, social stalking?

Part A: Basic Demographic and Background Information

1. Name
2. Gender
3. Age
4. City
5. Job
6. Previous jobs
7. Title or label (e.g., mother, daughter, pianist, etc.)
8. Marital status
9. Kids
10. Favorite books, music, TV shows, podcasts, movies
11. Magazines they read
12. Favorite celebrities
13. Favorite authors, mentors, writers, speakers
14. Brands they love
15. Events or conferences they attend
16. Things they do in their free time
17. Their guilty pleasures
18. Social media accounts they follow
19. *And the list could go on, and on ...*

Part B: Behavioral Desires, Needs, Jobs, and Challenges

1. Jobs they want to get done. *(More on that in Chapter 2: What Do They Want to Do?)*
2. Dreams, ambitions, and desires. *(More on that in Chapter 3: Why Do They Want to Do It?)*
3. Challenges. *(More on that in Chapter 4: What Is Stopping Them?)*

Each of these items gives you a peek into the needs and desires of the potential customers that you want to serve and gives you clues on how to meet their needs. **Part A: "Basic Demographic and Background Information"** will provide you with details you could use to pin down your customers, starting from who you want to interview to ultimately reaching them through targeted advertisements so they will buy your products. And, as you read through the book, you will learn how to uncover more customer insights in **Part B: "Behavioral Desires, Needs, Jobs, and Challenges,"** which you will use to fine-tune your product to find that perfect fit with your market's needs, making your market yell, "Here ... Take my money!"

Think of the list above as a starting point. Then, feel free to add, update, or delete any items to fit your project needs.

Tip

Don't worry too much about populating **Part B: 'Behavioral Desires, Needs, Jobs, and Challenges'** right now. We will go further into detail about it in the upcoming chapters. You can update it as you go.

The details you gather about your persona are usually populated on a persona card so that you can always refer to that customer whenever you are ideating, creating, or testing products that fit their needs. Here is an example of how a persona card could look as you fill it out.

PART A	PART B

NAME: Sally

FEMALE 30 YEARS OLD
DUBAI ENGAGED

BACKGROUND:

Sally works for an advertising agency with minimal time to get ready in the morning but must look absolutely stunning because her client-facing job depends on her image. She wants to look professional yet feminine. More importantly, she wants to feel like herself. Sally buys everything online, even groceries. She doesn't have enough time to cook but still tries to stay fit and healthy. Sally enjoys going out for social gatherings to connect and network with other people.

QUOTE:

"When you are stuck, walk away from the computer and draw. It will teach you how to see." - **Gerard Huerta**

JOB:
Creative Director

FAVORITE BOOKS:
The Alchemist, Harry Potter

FAVORITE MOVIES:
Batman, Iron Man

FAVORITE MAGAZINES:
Vogue, Cosmopolitan

EVENTS & CONFERENCES:
Future of Branding Week, Creative Works, World Domination Summit

BRANDS SHE LOVES:
Louis Vuitton, Zara, Apple

GUILTY PLEASURES:
Chips, Diet Coke

JOBS SHE IS TRYING TO DO:
- Dress professionally
- Buy groceries
- Cook healthy food
- Exercise
- Go out for social gatherings and network
- Connect with her fiancé and have a healthy relationship

DREAMS, AMBITIONS & DESIRES:
- Look professional
- Feel beautiful
- Be admired by her colleagues
- Stay fit and look healthy
- Have a supportive community
- Have a loving relationship

FEARS & CHALLENGES:
- Being perceived as unprofessional
- Not getting the promotion she has been waiting for
- Gaining weight
- Having limited time to do all the things she wants to to
- Missing out on special gatherings

BUYING INFLUENCE

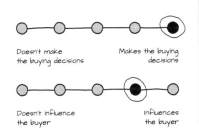

Persona Card Sample

Empathy Map:

Now that you have started to visualize your own version of Sally based on the above persona card, let's move forward with a simple exercise to help you understand what she is feeling called **The Empathy Map**.

> **The Empathy Map** helps you empathize with your customer. You see, it's one thing to know who they are and what they do for a living, but it's quite another to put yourself in their shoes, to try and truly feel how they feel and think how they think. Ultimately, that's what will help you speak to their needs and create products that help them either solve a problem they have or make their lives easier by doing certain things faster and better.

Don't worry too much if you don't have all the answers now. You might be thinking, *"How the heck should I know what they are feeling?"* We will cover this more in depth throughout later chapters of this book.

The idea here is to get you started. And remember, this is an iterative and continuous process. You can always come back and fine-tune your persona as you learn more about her.

How to populate an Empathy Map

1. Select a persona. Then, gather your team and brief them about your persona and her background. Include all the excellent work you have done to populate the persona card.
2. Divide the circle into sections:
   - Seeing – What are they seeing?

- Hearing – What are they hearing?
- Saying – What are they saying?
- Doing – What are they doing?
- Thinking and Feeling – What are they thinking? What are they feeling?
  - Pains – What is keeping them up at night?
  - Gains – What makes them happy?

3. Ask each member of your team to describe their own experience from the persona's point of view.
4. Collect your team's feedback and communicate it back to them.

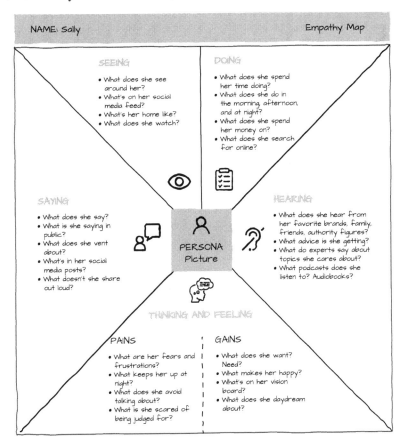

Empathy Map

Tips:

- It's best to include team members in this exercise who directly interact and engage with your customers. That way, you have great preliminary insight into what customers feel.
- Ask everyone on the team to conduct online research to get real insights into the persona-a.k.a. social stalking. Check online forums, Facebook personal feeds or Groups, YouTube, online comments, online magazines, and all different sorts of social media outlets, etc. You will find a wealth of information to help you build an Empathy Map, not from your head but from your market. (Refer to qualitative research in the next section.)

 **Sherwette**
@Sherwette

Asking your customers about their situation is the golden standard, but the second-best thing to do is listen to what they are saying on social media.

8:14 AM · 4 Feb, 2022

What's the output?

The Empathy Map helps you gain more insights into the needs and desires of your persona. The outputs of this exercise will be used further down the line when you want to come up with and test your product's value proposition. I'll use the Sally example to show how the Empathy Map is used to determine whether your product aligns with your persona's goals:

- Does my product really help alleviate Sally's pain when she is struggling in the morning to prepare a healthy breakfast with very little time? Which feature eases this specific pain?
- What can I do to go above and beyond to delight Sally with a service that will make her life easier?

(More on that in Chapter 5: What Problem Are You Helping Them Solve?)

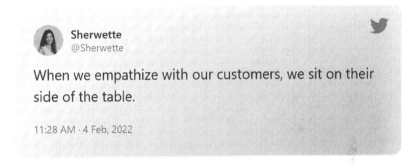

Sherwette
@Sherwette

When we empathize with our customers, we sit on their side of the table.

11:28 AM · 4 Feb, 2022

Customer Research: *How do you populate the persona card?*

You have one of two approaches, or a third if you decide to use a hybrid of the two. In the next section, we'll discuss which research method works best for you.

What are the types of research?
- **Qualitative Research** - Firsthand, natural data collection; non-numerical
- **Quantitative Research** - Numerical data and statistical measurements
- **Hybrid** - Combination of the two types for the sake of gathering the most insight

Approach 1: Qualitative/Lean Approach

The first approach involves collecting this information using a lean approach where you will be using one or more qualitative research methods.

Qualitative research is exploratory and nonnumerical. It is used to gain a deep contextual understanding of customers and usually is focused on smaller sample sizes than quantitative research. It is used to reveal customers' attitudes, behaviors, underlying reasons, opinions, motivations, and hidden factors. These are all insights that help you build better products.

Qualitative research is used to uncover trends and dive deeper into the problem. It helps you develop hypotheses that can potentially be confirmed.

Examples include conducting phone interviews, face-to-face interviews, focus groups (group discussions), observations, open-ended questionnaires, online chatting, and even social stalking.

"There are also unknown unknowns, things we don't know we don't know." -Donald Rumsfeld

Approach 2: Quantitative Approach

The second approach is collecting information using the Quantitative Method of Research. It is used to quantify the problem and generate numerical data that is usable in a statistical format. It uses data to formalize facts and uncover patterns of customers' attitudes, opinions, and behaviors. It is more structured than qualitative methods and is usually used to confirm a qualitative research hypothesis.

Examples include surveys (online and paper), online polls, systematic observations, and online user behavior analytics.

After you have identified your persona, and before doing any research to dig deeper into that persona, it's best to decide how much research is enough in order to be as efficient as possible. Throughout this decision process, you might ask yourself questions like:

Do I need to survey 1000 customers, or is 100 enough?

How many interviews do I need to conduct to gain good insights?

How many focus groups should I have?

Research Sample Size: *How much research is enough?*

How many interviews to conduct? How many surveys to fill?

More often than not, my clients think the more, the merrier. And, while having more significant numbers gives us a sense of comfort, it's not always necessary.

Following the qualitative approach, with a small number of interviews and focus groups, you can gain a wealth of insight at the same level that you would if you had doubled, tripled, or quadrupled that number. More is not always better. Larger numbers can still give you the same results. The same goes for the quantitative approach. You don't need thousands of respondents on your survey to gain valuable insights that you can rely on.

Let's talk about that for a bit, shall we?

Approach 1: Qualitative/Lean Approach

I remember one client once asked to conduct 47 focus groups targeting the same exact customer segment. Forty-seven is a huge number for focus groups, and it would take a long time to conduct them all. The excellent news is that you don't need 47 focus groups if you decide to follow the lean qualitative approach.

How much is enough?

There have been multiple debates on what the right sample size is for qualitative research. To determine the sample size for your qualitative research, you have to use saturation as a guiding principle. Saturation is when conducting any further analysis will not bring you any more valuable insight than if you had just kept the smaller sample size.

The number of interviews required for saturation to occur will depend on the nature of the topic being researched. The more niche or specialized the research topic is, the higher the sample size is required to reach saturation.

As per Daniel Bertaux's guidelines which are in favor of the more economical approach,[1] fifteen is the smallest sample size required for qualitative research regardless of the method.

That being said, some research may require a sample size as little as six to achieve enough saturation, which is driven mainly by the uniformity or similarity of the population size.

An average of ten responses usually brings you the level of insight you need in your quest to learn more about your customer.

Approach 2: Quantitative Approach

The quantitative approach is a bit simpler. You design the survey once and send it to your customers. It also helps you have access to a high confidence level from a statistical perspective.

There are a few terms you need to be familiar with before we go any further.

- **Population Size:** This is the number of people in the group you are trying to understand. For example, if you target the female population in the Middle East with curly hair, then the number of all females with curly hair in the Middle East is your population size.
- **Sample Size:** This is the number of customers who completed responses to your survey.
- **Confidence Level Percentage:** This percentage tells you how confident you can be that the population will select an answer within a specific range. For example, a 95% confidence level means that you can be 95% certain that the results will be within a specific range.
- **The Margin of Error Percentage:** This percentage tells you the amount of random sampling error in your survey results. The larger the margin of error, the less confident you will be in the survey. The smaller the margin of error, the closer you are to having a high confidence level.[2]

You can follow this formula to identify the confidence level associated with the number of responses. If math is not your thing, there are plenty of online calculators you can use (see below). For example, the sample size calculator by Survey Monkey can be found at https://www.surveymonkey.com/mp/sample-size-calculator/.

$$\text{Sample size:} \quad \cfrac{\dfrac{z^2 \times p\,(1-p)}{e^2}}{1+\left(\cfrac{z^2 \times p\,(1-p)}{e^2 N}\right)}$$

N = population size

e = Margin of error (percentage in decimal form)

z = z-score, representing the size of the confidence interval you have set, measured in units of standard deviations from the mean

Desired confidence level	z-score
80%	1.28
85%	1.44
90%	1.65
95%	1.96
99%	2.58

As I mentioned before, there are many online calculators to choose from that can help you figure out the sample based on the confidence level you are looking for. So don't worry about putting that formula into a spreadsheet!

Ideally, your confidence level should not be less than 95%. This means that there is a 95% chance that the analysis result did not happen by accident.

Let's say that your **population size is 100,000,** and you want to figure out the sample size where the **margin of error is 5%.**

Based on the confidence level, you must gather a certain number of responses as shown below:

Population Size	Margin of Error %	Confidence Level %	Sample Size
100,000	5%	90%	270
100,000	5%	**95%**	**383**
100,000	5%	99%	660

If you go with the standard **confidence level** of **95%**, then your **sample size** is **383**. The higher number of responses you get, the higher the confidence level is in your analysis.

Research Approach Selection: *Which research method should you choose?*

Each approach gives you a different kind of insight, so I would suggest doing both. If you don't have a list or customer database to send surveys to, you can gain a wealth of insight using the lean or qualitative approach. Usually, it gives you more insight than you would have thought.

Think about this. People love to talk about themselves. When you open the floor for them to talk about their challenges, they will give you gold.

The quantitative approach helps you obtain data that you can confidently use. However, it does limit the number of customer insights you could potentially tap into. For example, suppose you want to dive deep into a specific topic. You want to start with the qualitative methods and then focus your quantitative survey on validating the most pressing hypotheses. Remember, people hate filling out surveys. If it takes more than two minutes, they are less likely to do it unless they are getting paid for it.

Use the qualitative approach for defining the persona and getting the insights required. Quantitative is better suited when we want to validate a hypothesis, such as in the testing phase *(More on that in Chapter 7: Are You Really Helping Them?)*, and gain confidence when deciding to scale.

Here is a quick cheat sheet on the differences between the two approaches:

Qualitative vs. Quantitative Research Methods Cheat Sheet

	Qualitative	Quantitative
Purpose	Understanding the "why" and uncovering insights about motivations, opinions, and attitudes. It is used to form an initial hypothesis.	Understanding the "what," "where," and "when" of the customers' needs and problems. It is used to confirm hypotheses formed in qualitative research.
Methods	Loosely structured to gain contextual information, such as focus groups or interviews.	Highly structured to gather data about what customers do and find related patterns, such as online surveys.
Sample size *(Refer to the section: Research Sample Size: How much research is enough research?)*	Smaller	Larger
Statistical Reliability	Not statistically reliable. Be wary of projecting your personal bias based on the insights outputs.	Statistically reliable based on the number of customers evaluated.

Chapter Quiz

Congratulations on making it through the first chapter! At this point, you should know who your customer is, have decided on your research methods, and stalked your customer a little (or maybe a little too much!) to uncover their needs. Be sure to check the next page for the "Putting It All into Action" section of this chapter.

Ready to test your knowledge with a chapter quiz?

True/False

1: The more customer research you do, the better. You should always strive to get as many responses as you can. If you are running a survey, you need thousands of responses to ensure your results are reliable. (True/False)

2: Qualitative research is better than quantitative research. (True/False)

<u>Quiz Answer Key</u>

Answer 1: False. More research is not always better. Whether you have decided to use qualitative or quantitative research methods, the correct number of respondents will be determined by achieving a saturation level. Qualitative research may range from 6 to 15 responses. In quantitative research, it depends on the confidence level and margin of error you are comfortable with.

Answer 2: False. No one form of research is better than the other. You may decide the method that best suits your research needs based on the purpose of that research. For example, qualitative methods will give you a wealth of insight into a specific customer segment or problem statement. On the other hand, if you're going to validate a hypothesis before scaling, you may wish to use quantitative research methods.

Putting It All into Action

Now that you have learned about knowing your customer, it's time to get down to business and put it all into action.

I know you're tempted to flip this page and read the next chapter. If you want to do so, then by all means, go for it. Who am I to stop you? Still, I encourage you to give it a try and work on these exercises. This is the most important chapter of all chapters. If you don't know your customer, everything else might as well turn to ashes. I know because I was just like you, tempted to learn more before executing. Trust the process. Clarity comes from engagement, and it will all make more sense once you do the work. So first, let's finish this chapter, shall we?

If you are still tempted to read more, be sure to go back and do these exercises. They are so important!

Here's your checklist:

1. Identify the persona you are targeting.
2. Fill in the persona card. **(Part A: Basic and Background Information)**
3. Continue to fill in the persona card details as you go through the content of this book. **(Part B: Behavioral Desires, Needs, Jobs, and Challenges)**
4. Gather your team and populate the Empathy Map.

5. Decide on whether you are going to use:
   - Qualitative research approach.
   - Quantitative research approach.
   - A hybrid of qualitative and quantitative research approaches.
6. Start researching and talking to your customers.

Great job accomplishing all your goals for Chapter 1! You're well on your way to creating products and services your customers will love, buy, and use! In Chapter 2, we'll be discussing the jobs your customers are attempting to accomplish so that you can help them do those jobs better and faster.

<u>References</u>

1. Daniel Bertaux. Essay. "In a Very Different Picture." The Life-History Approach to the Transformation of Sociological Practice, 29–45. 1978.
2. "Sample Size Calculator: UNDERSTANDING Sample Sizes." SurveyMonkey, December 6, 2016. https://www.surveymonkey.com/mp/sample-size-calculator/.

CHAPTER 2

What Do They Want to Do?

*"If I had asked people what they wanted,
they would have said faster horses."*
—Henry Ford

Chapter Objectives:

- **Jobs-to-be-Done**: What are Jobs-to-be-Done?
- **Jobs-to-be-Done Case Study**: Milkshake sales for a fast-food chain.
- **Jobs-to-be-Done Statement**: How do you put together a jobs-to-be-done statement?
- **Case Study**: Hair Addict Product - The Indian Recipe

When it comes to innovation and creating new products or services, we tend to only consider what is familiar to *us*.

You might think, *"I want to create something that I would really want, something I am passionate about."*

While your passion is crucial for keeping you going, it might not necessarily be what your customers want.

There are two main schools of thought when it comes to creating new products:

1. **Ideation:** Ideate, brainstorm, test as many ideas as you can, and fail fast.
2. **Needs and Challenges:** Find out about your customers' needs and then cater to those needs.

1] Ideation: Ideate, brainstorm, test as many ideas as you can, and fail fast.

Many entrepreneurs and product designers adopt this approach.

When you fail, and fail fast, it means you have burned far less money than what you could have lost.

While that actually sounds good, what sounds even better is to fail less than to fail fast.

Failing fast still costs a lot of money.

We might think of ourselves as great ideators, but as much as we want to feed our egos, it's best to accept that the ideas we come up with might not fit what our customers really want.

As Tony Ulwick mentioned in his book *Jobs-to-be-Done* (JTBD),[1] there are three reasons why the idea-first approach isn't very effective.

1. More ideas doesn't necessarily mean one of them will help and satisfy your customers.
2. If you don't know your customers' needs and desires, you can miss out on great ideas and end up with bad ones.
3. Customers don't have the answers. They don't know what they need. They are not scientists, engineers, or researchers and therefore can't give you solutions.

Customers can, however, tell you about their challenges, desires, motivations, and dreams.

2] Needs and Challenges - Find out about your customers' needs, then serve them.

Many entrepreneurs and product designers do recognize this approach. They talk to their customers and ask them about their challenges, seeking to understand their underlying motivations for doing what they do. More importantly, they figure out what it is that they actually do.

But as Henry Ford said, *"If I had asked people what they wanted, they would have said faster horses."*

What does this mean?

It means it's not enough to ask customers about their challenges or their needs. You need to dig deeper and understand the motivation behind certain actions. Only then will you truly understand what your customers want to do when faced with a specific scenario. You have to know what success means to your customer.

Your customers buy products or services for either one of two reasons:

1. **Reason #1:** They will help them <u>achieve their goals in a better way</u>. In other words, this product or service will help them do a job that they currently do better and faster.
2. **Reason #2:** They will help them <u>overcome a challenge they are currently facing</u>.

Expert Tip:

> *"Customer needs, either expressed or yet-to-be-articulated, provide new product development opportunities for the firm."* -The Product Development Management Association (PDMA)[2]

So, which approach are you following?

Jobs-to-be-Done: *What are "Jobs-to-be-Done?"*

Jobs-to-be-done are what customers actually do. It's the action they take. For example: Drilling a screw into the wall. That's the job.

> **Jobs-to-be-done** refers to what your customer is trying to get done. It could be a routine, a specific task, an action she wants to complete, a need or desire she wants to fulfill, a challenge she wants to overcome, or a problem she is looking to solve. It's what she wants to do.

Learning about the actual job the customer is doing will intrigue you to know more. Perhaps the customer doesn't have any issues putting a screw into the wall. She might even enjoy it and offer to help her friends with such a task.

You start learning more when you understand "why" she is drilling the screw into the wall in the first place. Maybe it's because she wants to hang a frame, a clock, or even her big TV.

So, start thinking. To drill the screw into the wall, she would need to have a drill. If she doesn't have one, she is left with a problem. Maybe she doesn't want to buy a drill just to hang one mirror on the wall. Perhaps she has a drill, but all she wants to do is hang one small picture frame, so she wonders if it's worth ruining the wall for it. What if she wanted to remove it later on? What if she doesn't quite fancy the position of the frame after hanging it? Or, what if hammering in a nail would work better instead?

You see, the job itself, hanging something up on the wall, may or may not be the issue. Once you clarify the jobs that your ideal customer—your "perfect person"—wants to do, you can start to form your thinking process to help them:

1. Do the job faster and better.
2. Remove the obstacles keeping them from doing the job-to-be-done.

Many people say, *"I need a car."* It's said more often than you think, especially where I originally come from, Cairo: the city of chaos. (It's a gripping driving experience, to say the least.) On the other hand, people who live in London or Paris barely even think of having a car, let alone say, *"I need a car."*

The question we want to think about here for a moment is **whether or not these people** *actually* **need a car.** Or, is it that they think they need a car because it will help them fulfill a purpose, or *job,* that they don't think they can fulfill without a personal vehicle?

Do they really need a car?

No, they don't. They "need" to get a job done.

They *need* a car because it takes them from point A to point B, and if they had an alternative method that was easier and faster than a car, then they wouldn't really "need" a car anymore.

The job they want to do is get from point A to point B. Therefore, the perception of needing a car is limited to the thought that this is the only convenient and cost-effective method of transportation to fulfill that job.

Understanding the jobs-to-be-done by your customers will help you uncover their true motivations and direct you on the path to fulfilling their needs.

"The focus should not be on what products customers want, but on what jobs they are trying to get done." - Tony Ulwick, Founder of Strategyn[3]

Jobs-to-be-Done Case Study: *Milkshake Sales for a Fast-Food Chain*

To drive this point home, here is an example shared by Professor Clayton Christensen of a real-case scenario in which a fast-food company uses jobs-to-be-done to increase the sales of a milkshake.[4]

The fast-food company first followed the classic approach of market research to improve their milkshake recipe. They started out by speaking to their target market to learn about their milkshake preferences. Then, they tried to make the milkshake chocolaty-er, chunkier, and chewier. They adjusted the formula multiple times with no luck. They even tried making it cheaper, but their sales didn't increase.

Nothing they did worked.

That is, until they had their jobs-to-be-done analyzed and focused on helping their customers do their jobs better. So, how did they do this?

They started observing the customers in the restaurant for 18 hours a day and pinpointed those who were buying that particular milkshake. As it turned out, half of them were adults who had shown up alone at around 8 a.m. just before a long drive to work.

The next day, in their own words, the fast-food chain asked those customers, *"What 'job' were you trying to do for yourself that caused you to come here and 'hire' that milkshake?"*

One would think, what is the job of a milkshake anyway? To stave off hunger? Make the customer feel good? Most people think milkshakes are just for kids ... But just hold on. These are only assumptions. This is why it's so important to understand your customers and do proper customer research. *(Refer to Chapter 1: Who Do You Want to Serve? and Chapter 3: Why Do They Want to Do It?)*

As we dig deeper into the jobs-to-be-done, we can see that the job of the milkshake was to:

Be breakfast on the way to work as it was easy to consume and wouldn't spill on the customer's clothes.

Entertain the customer during their long drive to work being that it was something to sip on.

Fill up the customer's stomach so they wouldn't feel hungry by 10 a.m.

> *"When people find themselves needing to get a job done, they essentially hire products to do that job for them."*
> -Clayton Christensen[5]

And so, the research tells a story:

A bunch of adults went to a fast-food chain to buy milkshakes for breakfast. They wanted to be entertained on the way to work. They could continue to look sharp when they arrived at the office because they wouldn't be ruining their nice outfits with drops of chocolate from their favorite donuts, which would have been the alternative. Most importantly, they didn't want to feel hungry by 10 a.m.

Changing the milkshake formula wouldn't have helped the customer do these jobs any better. How do we know?

This is the milkshake's competition according to the customers interviewed:

#	The Milkshake's Competition	Challenge
1	Donut	It would have made a mess on their clothes.
2	Sandwich	It would have been hard to eat while driving.
3	Bananas	It would have caused a sudden urge to use the bathroom.
4	Bagel	It would have been too dry and tasteless.
5	Snickers	They would have felt guilty after eating it.

These were the customers' objections to the other products they would have hired to do the same job as the fast-food milkshake. You see, it wasn't another milkshake from a competitor fast-food chain that was competing for the job. This list is made up of entirely different products that you wouldn't usually think of as competition for a milkshake.

So, what would have made the milkshake do its job better so that customers would love it and buy more of it?

Guess what? All that the customers wanted was for the milkshake to last longer.

This was achieved by making the straw slimmer and the milkshake thicker so that customers could sip on it longer while on the road.

AND BAM! Just like that, sales skyrocketed.

How fascinating is that?

So, you see, when the customers' real jobs, pains, and gains were revealed, one little tweak made the product do the job better and created more profits.

Expert Tip:

"If a [businessperson] can understand the job, design a product and associated experiences in purchase and use to do that job, and deliver it in a way that reinforces its intended use, then when customers find themselves needing to get that job done, they will hire that product." -Clayton Christensen[6]

The milkshake story is excellent in that it provides a thought-provoking perspective on market research and competitive analysis. If you want to hear the story firsthand from Professor Clayton Christensen, you can do so by watching a 4-minute video on YouTube.

YouTube link:
https://www.youtube.com/watch?v=sfGtw2C95Ms&t=41s

Alternatively, you can read the transcript here.

The Milkshake Story on Jobs-to-be-Done

We actually hire products to do things for us. And understanding what job we have to do in our lives for which we would hire a product is really the key to cracking this problem of motivating customers to buy what we're offering.

So I wanted just to tell you a story about a project we did for one of the big fast-food restaurants. They were trying to goose up the sales of their milkshakes. They had just studied this problem up the gazoo. They brought in customers who fit the profile of the quintessential milkshake consumer. They'd give them samples and ask, "Could you tell us how we could improve our milkshakes so you'd buy more of them? Do you want it chocolaty-er, cheaper, chunkier, or chewier?"

They'd get very clear feedback and they'd improve the milkshake on those dimensions and it had no impact on sales or profits whatsoever.

So one of our colleagues went in with a different question on his mind. And that was, "I wonder what job arises in people's lives that causes them to come to this restaurant to hire a milkshake?" We stood in a restaurant for 18 hours one day and just took very careful data. What time did they buy these milkshakes? What were they wearing? Were they alone? Did they buy other food with it? Did they eat it in the restaurant or drive off with it?

It turned out that nearly half of the milkshakes were sold before 8 o'clock in the morning. The people who bought them were always alone. It was the only thing they bought, and they all got in the car and drove off with it.

To figure out what job they were trying to hire it to do, we came back the next day and stood outside the restaurant so we could confront these folks as they left milkshake-in-hand. And in language that they could understand, we essentially asked, "Excuse me please, but I gotta sort this puzzle out. What job were you trying to do for yourself that caused you to come here and hire that milkshake?"

They'd struggle to answer, so we then helped them by asking other questions like, "Well, think about the last time you were in the same situation needing to get the same job done, but you didn't come here to hire a milkshake. What did you hire?"

And then, as we put all their answers together, it became clear that they all had the same job to be done in the morning. That is that they had a long and boring drive to work, and they just needed something to do while they drove to keep the commute interesting. One hand had to be on the wheel, but someone had given them another hand, and there wasn't anything in it. And they just needed something to do when they drove. They weren't hungry yet, but they knew they would be hungry by 10 o'clock, so they also wanted something that would just plunk down there and stay for their morning.

The milkshake buyer:

"Good question. What do I hire when I do this job? You know, I've never framed the question that way before, but last Friday, I hired a banana to do the job. Take my word for it. Never hire bananas. They're gone in three minutes—you're hungry by 7:30 am. If you promise not to tell my wife, I probably hire donuts twice a week, but they don't do it well either. They're gone fast. They crumb all over my clothes. They get my fingers gooey. Sometimes I hire bagels but as you know, they're so dry and tasteless. Then I have to steer the car with my knees while I'm putting jam on it, and if the phone rings, we got a crisis. I remember I hired a Snickers bar once, but I felt so guilty I've never hired Snickers again. Let me tell you, when I hire this milkshake, it is so viscous that it easily takes me 20 minutes to suck it up through that thin little straw. Who cares what the ingredients are—I don't. All I know is I'm full all morning, and it fits right here in my cupholder."

Conclusion:

Well, it turns out that the milkshake does the job better than any of the competitors, which in the customer's minds are not Burger King milkshakes but bananas, donuts, bagels, Snickers bars, coffee, and so on.

I hope you can see how if you understand the job, improving the product just becomes obvious.

Jobs-to-be-Done Statement: *How do you put together a Jobs-to-be-Done Statement?*

Think of the following phrase for your customer:

When (situation), I want to (JOB: motivations & forces) so that I can (expected outcome [desire]).

In the milkshake scenario, the statement could be the following:

When I go to work every day **(situation), I want to** have breakfast **(motivations & forces) so that I can** enjoy my ride, stay full, and continue to look professional by the time I arrive at work **(expected outcome [desire]).**

Let's dissect each of the components of this phrase.

1] Situation: When (situation), I want to (JOB: motivations & forces) so that I can (expected outcome [desire]).

This is when the customer is "triggered" to do a specific job. For example, in the milkshake scenario, the customer is triggered to think about breakfast during the long drive to work.

2] Motivations & Forces: When (situation), **I want to (JOB: motivations & forces)** so that I can (expected outcome [desire]).

This is the job that the customer wants to do once triggered by that specific situation, such as driving to work.

There are different kinds of jobs-to-be-done, as explained by Tony Ulwick in his book, *Jobs-to-be-Done*:[7]

1. **Core Functional Job** – The main job your customer wants to do. For example: have breakfast, grow their hair, make coffee, listen to music, or clean their house. The core functional job has a few characteristics and should apply to all jobs:
    *   A job is stable; it doesn't change over time.
    *   A job has no geographical boundaries.
    *   A job is solution-agnostic.
2. **Related Job** – A job that helps accomplish the core functional job. For example, if I am making coffee, I am also getting a mug to pour my coffee into in order to drink it.
3. **Emotional Job** – The job that defines how your customers want to feel or avoid feeling. For example, if I grow my hair long and soft, it will make me feel confident.
4. **Social Job** – The job that defines how your customers want to be perceived by others. For example, if I grow my hair long and soft, men will see me as attractive. Another example of this would be a businessman buying a fancy car to be seen as prestigious.
5. **Consumption Chain Jobs** – All the jobs you have to do to take care of the product you bought throughout its lifecycle. For example, if you want to make coffee, the following jobs will revolve around it:
    *   Going to the supermarket
    *   Buying coffee
    *   Putting the coffee in the coffee container
    *   Storing coffee in the kitchen
    *   Cleaning the coffee machine

- Putting the coffee in the coffee machine
- Making coffee *(core functional job)*
- Pouring coffee into your favorite mug *(related job)*

Products are bought to do the core job; for example, *making coffee.* However, in the process of buying, delivering, using, repairing, cleaning, maintaining, and disposing of the product—in this case, the coffee machine—there are numerous related and consumption jobs that need to be done, too. Many questions must be answered. *Who is buying the coffee? From where? How is she making the coffee? Where are the beans coming from? Is she using a machine or pot? If she is using a coffee machine, which one? Does it require capsules? If yes, where could she buy these capsules? How often should she buy them? And are they going to break the bank? How often should the coffee machine be cleaned? What happens if it stops working and requires maintenance?* And the list goes on.

3] Expected Outcome: When (situation), I want to (JOB: motivations & forces) **so that I can (expected outcome [desire]).**

This is the desired outcome or the definition of what success looks like for your customer. In the milkshake scenario, it's to feel full, not mess up the work outfit, and be entertained during the long drive.

One way to figure out the desired outcomes is to think, *"Why does a customer want to do this job?" (More on that in Chapter 3: Why Do They Want to Do It?)*

Emotional and social jobs are powerful jobs, and even though they are not the main or "core" jobs, they hit on your customers' desires. Therefore, they could essentially be considered outcomes of their own and align closely with the eight basic needs and wants of the human being. *(More on that in Chapter 3: Why Do They Want to Do It?)*

Let's have a look, shall we?

Eight Basic Needs and Wants and the Emotional and Social Jobs

Eight Basic Needs and Wants	Emotional Job	Social Job
Survival	Yes	
Food and Drink	Yes	
Freedom from Fear, Pain, and Danger	Yes	
Sexual Companionship	Yes	Yes
Comfortable Living Conditions	Yes	Yes
To Be Superior	Yes	Yes
Care and Protection of Loved Ones	Yes	Yes
Social Approval	Yes	Yes

Once you have determined the emotional and social jobs you customer wishes to achieve, you will be able to tap into your customers' motivations.

Another way to figure out your customers' expected outcomes is to simply ask yourself, *"What does 'success' mean to my customer?"*

A specific outcome is the **measurement or metric** that your customer will use to measure the level of success and satisfaction with the job she just did. For example, if the job is to make coffee, the expected outcome is to enjoy the coffee. However, if the coffee she just made doesn't taste very good, then the desired outcome has failed according to the success metric your customer has identified.

Another example would be if I spent 100 dollars on vitamins to grow my hair, diligently taking them three times a day every day for three months and my hair doesn't grow to the expected length, I would be disappointed.

Expert Tip:

> "While defining the functional job correctly is important, uncovering the customer's desired outcomes (the metrics they use to measure success when getting the job done) is the real key to success at innovation."
> -Tony Ulwick[8]

Financial Outcomes

Now that we have covered outcomes that fulfill emotional and social jobs, we must not forget about financial outcomes. The tricky thing is that the financial outcomes do not always necessarily reflect on the person who is doing the core job.

The financial outcome is one major deciding factor the buyer goes through in her mind before deciding to buy. While one person might be making the coffee, someone else might be buying the coffee machine.

The person buying the coffee machine is more invested in making mental calculations. They might say to themselves, *"This coffee machine is expensive, but I'll be saving money by making coffee at home, as opposed to buying two or three Starbucks coffees a day."* It might seem like a big purchase the buyer has to make at first, but in the long run, it has a good return on investment for the buyer.

Case Study: *Hair Addict Product - The Indian Recipe*

Let me tell you a little bit about one of my very favorite emerging products for hair growth. It's called *The Indian Recipe* by **The Hair Addict.**[9]

The Hair Addict is a startup that I absolutely adore. The founder, Doaa Gawish, has a passion for hair, specifically curly hair and natural hair remedies. She created a line of products that help you grow your hair faster than usual, like *The Indian Recipe,* as well as other products that protect your hair from things like swimming pool chlorine and sea salt. She also sells other products to help you care for your hair, such as silk pillows, special towels to keep your curls frizz-free, hair diffusers, and hair picks.

For this example, I want to focus on one of her products, *The Indian Recipe.*

You apply the product 2-3 times a week on your hair roots for 3-6 months. Then, you witness incredible results in the rate of your hair growth. Having had short hair for a very long time (since I was born, actually), I always dreamt of having long hair. And so, a friend recommended this recipe to me.

When I first learned about it, there was no product to buy. They didn't even have a website or store.

So, what was there?

There was a Facebook Group called **The Hair Addict** (https://www.facebook.com/groups/530733733775051) ... and at the time of writing this book in September 2021, it currently has 236K+ members.

What was in that group?

Conversations about how to create this remedy at home from scratch, including all the ingredients and proportions, where to get the ingredients, and how to make the remedy yourself.

Here is a personal #confession:

I personally went through the trouble of trying to buy all the ingredients, only to fail miserably while trying to mix all the right proportions.

What can I say? Not everyone is great at mixing ingredients properly, and that's why I became the perfect customer to buy the recipe in its ready-made off-the-shelf form to apply to my hair and see magical results right away.

Fast forward to today, September 2021, *The Indian Recipe* is mass-produced, available to buy online and from specific salons, with plans to be available as an off-the-shelf product to a wider market.

Jobs-to-be-Done Example:

If we want to apply the Jobs-to-be-Done methodology to *The Hair Addict*, this could be one of the scenarios:

When (situation), I want to (JOB: motivations & forces) so that I can (expected outcome [desire]).

In one year, I want to grow my hair to look more attractive and feel confident.

1. **Core Functional Job** – The main job your customer wants to do.
    - Case study: I want to grow my hair.
2. **Related Job** – The job that helps get more jobs done.
    - Case study: I want to apply the hair treatment every week to grow my hair. I want to buy all the tools, vitamins, and treatments that will help me grow my hair.
3. **Emotional Job** – The job that defines how your customers want to feel or avoid feeling.
    - Case study: Longer hair will make me feel more confident and attractive.
4. **Social Job** – The job that defines how your customers want to be perceived by others
    - Case study: People will compliment me on my longer, more gorgeous hair, and as I feel more confident, I will socialize more with other people.
5. **Consumption Chain Jobs** – All the jobs the customer has to do to take care of the product they bought throughout its lifecycle

- Case study: *The Indian Recipe* is now available as a product to buy and apply right away; however, before it was available, customers would have to buy all the ingredients, mix it up, and prepare it themselves before applying it to their hair. So, as a customer, what do I have to do in both scenarios?
- **Scenario A: Buy ingredients and prepare the recipe.**
  - Go to the supermarket or other stores that sell the ingredients
  - Buy all ingredients for the treatment
  - Read the treatment recipe
  - Make the recipe
  - Apply the recipe to my hair for three hours
  - Wash my hair
  - Store the recipe in the fridge
  - Repeat
- **Scenario B: Buy the ready-made off-the-shelf product from the Hair Addict online store or any of the certified salons**
  - Go to one of the certified salons that sell the product, or go to the Hair Addict online store
  - Buy the pre-made recipe
  - Apply the recipe to my hair and leave it in for three hours
  - Wash my hair
  - Store the recipe in the fridge
  - Repeat
6. **Financial Jobs** – How much money the customer is going to spend or save.
   - Case study: I will save money on:

- Expensive vitamins
- Expensive advanced hair growth products
- Expensive treatments at the salon
- Expensive hair extensions
- Expensive treatments for my hair after having ruined it with hair extensions

Notice that for this product, 2/8 basic needs and wants are triggered. *(Refer to Chapter 3: Why Do They Want to Do It? for more details about the basic needs and wants.)*

Eight Basic Needs and Wants and the Emotional and Social Jobs for the Hair Addict

Eight Basic Needs and Wants	Emotional Job	Social Job
Survival	Yes	
Food and Drink	Yes	
Freedom from Fear, Pain, and Danger	Yes	
Sexual Companionship	Yes - Feel more confident and attractive (The Indian Recipe)	Yes - Be seen as attractive by the opposite gender (The Indian Recipe)
Comfortable Living Conditions	Yes	Yes
To Be Superior	Yes	Yes
Care and Protection of Loved Ones	Yes	Yes
Social Approval	Yes - Feel more confident and attractive (The Indian Recipe)	Yes - Be seen as attractive by others, and receive compliments (The Indian Recipe)

Chapter Quiz

Congratulations on making it through Chapter 2! You should now have an in-depth understanding of the jobs-to-be-done by your customers and how to put together a Jobs-to-be-Done Statement. Remember to check the next page for the "Putting It All into Action" section of this chapter.

Ready to test your knowledge with a chapter quiz?

True/False

1: A core job may have multiple related jobs that impact the customer who does the job. (True/False)

2: The customer who does the core job is always the one who cares about the financial outcomes. (True/False)

Quiz Answer Key

Answer 1: True. A core job may have multiple related, emotional, social, consumption chain, and financial jobs.

Answer 2: False. The customer who does the core job may or may not be the one who handles or is affected by the financial outcomes; for example, the decision-maker who decides which software to buy is not necessarily the one who will pay for it in the company. Another example would be the wife choosing a certain couch, but the husband might be the one paying for it.

Putting It All into Action

Now that you have learned about the jobs-to-be-done, it's time to put your observation goggles on and put it all into action.

1. Here's your checklist:
2. Identify the jobs-to-be-done by your target customer.
   - Categorize the jobs-to-be-done based on:
   - Core Job
   - Related Job
   - Emotional Job
   - Social Job
   - Consumption Chain Jobs
   - Financial Job
3. Map the emotional and social jobs to the eight basic needs and wants.

Woohoo! You are finished with Chapter 2! You are getting closer and closer to truly knowing your customers. What job does your customer want to do that you didn't think of before? In Chapter 3, we will be talking more about the desires that drive your customers to want to do those jobs in the first place.

References

1. Tony Ulwick. "Jobs-to-Be-Done: A Framework for Customer Needs." Medium. JTBD + Outcome-Driven Innovation, November 10, 2020. https://jobs-to-be-done.com/jobs-to-be-done-a-framework-for-customer-needs-c883cbf61c90.
2. "Glossary for New Product Development: A to H - PDMA." Product Development Management Association, n.d. https://www.pdma.org/page/glossary_access1.
3. Ulwick, "Jobs-to-Be-Done," 2020.
4. Clayton Christensen. "Clay Christensen's Jobs-to-be-Done Theory Framework." FullStory, April 9, 2020. https://www.fullstory.com/blog/clayton-christensen-jobs-to-be-done-framework-product-development.
5. Christensen, "Theory Framework," 2020.
6. Christensen, "Theory Framework," 2020.
7. Ulwick, "Jobs-to-Be-Done," 2020.
8. Ulwick, "Jobs-to-Be-Done," 2020.
9. Doaa Gawish. "The Indian Recipe - 100% Natural Hair Growth Product." The Hair Addict, n.d. https://thehairaddict.net/product/the-indian-recipe/.

CHAPTER 3

Why Do They Want to Do It?

"People don't want to buy a quarter-inch drill. They want a quarter-inch hole. But in fact, people rarely want a hole in the wall either; they want a comfortable living room."
—Theodore Levitt[1]

Chapter Objectives:

- **Consumers' Buying Triggers**: Why do you need to know why your customer wants to do that job?
- **Consumers' Motivations**: Why do your customers need to do the jobs they want to get done?
- **The 5 Whys Technique**: How do you know which biological triggers captivate your customers?
- **Dimensions of Desire and Its Strength**: Is it worth it for your business to pursue those desires?

Are you nosy?

If not, perhaps you should be.

In the previous chapter, you learned that your customer wants to do a specific job.

But why?

Take a moment and think about that phrase for a moment.

"People don't want to buy a quarter-inch drill. They want a quarter-inch hole."

—Theodore Levitt.

Do you even want a hole in your living room?

Imagine you moved to a new apartment, and you have a job to do. You want to drill a hole in the wall.

That's the core job.

And for you to do it, you need tools. You need a drill.

Why do you need a drill?

You need to drill the hole.

Why do you need there to be a hole in the wall?

You desire to have a beautiful home. Perhaps you wish to hang a TV, a mirror, a clock, or a painting. And each of these reasons for drilling a hole in the wall has an even more specific reason attached to it. The TV is for entertainment. The mirror is to make sure you look good. The clock is both practical and decorative.

Every reason has a different set of motivations and desires.

And if you dig even deeper, you can come up with new products that your customers would use to do the same job; for example, if you are hanging a clock or a painting nowadays, you don't need to drill a hole in the wall.

You can just buy some of those 3M Command damage-free wall hanging hooks. That way, if you want to move the location of your clock or your painting, you don't need to repaint your wall, saving you time, effort, and money.

Not bad.

Did you notice that the new product just did another job? It helped you avoid having to repaint your living room in the future.

Consumers' Buying Triggers: *Why do you need to know why your customer wants to do that job?*

You need to know why your customers do specific jobs. Now, you might be thinking, *Isn't it enough to just know what they do and help them do it better and more efficiently?*

In Chapter 2 *(What Do They Want to Do?)*, we touched on our customers' desires in our Jobs-to-be-Done Statement. Remember this?

When (situation), I want to (JOB: motivations & forces) so that I can (expected outcome [desire]).

Here is the example we used:

When I go to work every day **(situation),** I want to have breakfast **(motivations & forces)** so that I can enjoy my ride, stay full, and continue looking sharp by the time I arrive at work **(expected outcome[desire]).**

In specific situations, when a customer wants to do something, they wish to achieve a specific output. That output is the customer's desire, and if you don't identify that desire in the first place, you will find it harder to sell to your target customers.

Psychology Tip:

> If you want to sell, sell to 95% of the brain, which according to Harvard professor and author Gerald Zaltman, is not conscious. Our thoughts, emotions, and learning happen unconsciously, and we are not really aware of them.[2]

We like to think that we are rational, so when making major life decisions, we typically create a list of pros and cons; for example, in 2019, when I was deciding to change jobs, not only did I have a pros and cons list, but I gave a score for each item as a weighted percentage, then added my satisfaction level for each of those items. Although this logical model I had created voted against me leaving my previous job, I still went ahead and resigned.

I was hoping that my carefully designed model to help me decide would justify my decision to leave. It didn't.

Why did I change jobs even though my carefully designed rational model voted against it?

Sometimes, I still ask myself that question. I still don't have the answer. Our decisions are not rational.

One of my close friends often says to me, *"My dear Sherwette, not everything can be decided with an Excel sheet."* Although I believe her and know that we don't really make our decisions consciously, I still go ahead and create my pros and cons list with weighted averages against my satisfaction score to see which choice would make more sense to me. Why? A part of the brain wants that logical justification. We will dig deeper into this topic shortly.

> *"Although there are conscious and rational parts in most decisions, marketers need to focus first on appealing to the buyer's emotions and unconscious needs. It's not always bad to include factual details, as they will help the customer's logical brain justify the decision-just don't expect them to make the sale!"* - Roger Dooley.[3]

Many people perceive being emotional as a negative trait. They think that those who show their emotions to others are not in "control." They think you need to be composed, logical, and rational all the time.

That's what they think.

But even if "emotionally intact" people did a fantastic job of hiding their emotions, most of their actions would actually still be driven by emotions.

Let me show you why.

The Three Parts of the Brain

We all have three brains. Each plays a role when making decisions. **To sell, it's best to speak to all three of them.**

So ... What are these three brains?

1. **Old Brain (Reptilian/Lizard):** The survival brain, driven by our primal instincts that is on the lookout for survival and protection.
2. **Midbrain (Mammalian):** The emotional bit that drives your decisions; the happiness, anxiety, or sadness that drives your state of mind.
3. **New Brain (Neocortex):** The logical part of your brain that helps you make rational decisions.

1] The Old Brain (Reptilian/Lizard)

The old brain is all about our primitive instincts. It's about safety, survival, and sexuality.

"The lizard brain is hungry, scared, angry, and horny. The lizard brain only wants to eat and be safe. The lizard brain will fight (to the death) if it has to, but would rather run away. It likes a vendetta and has no trouble getting angry."-Seth Godin[4]

Our primitive instincts make us act without thinking and sometimes even without feeling. These instincts are impulsive, and the consequences could follow later.

If I asked you, "Would you ever stab someone?" what would you say?

Perhaps, your immediate reaction would be, *"What the heck? Are you crazy? What's wrong with you?"*

Maybe your response would be a little different, and you would tell me, *"It depends."*

And I do agree with you, it totally depends. It depends on the situation.

For example, what would you do if someone were trying to hurt or kidnap your daughter and you had a knife next to you?

Remember that famous scene from the movie *Taken* with Liam Neeson where he was determined to find his daughter no matter what and kill whoever was responsible for abducting her?

You see? The situation completely changes your judgment.

But our primitive instincts are not only about those life or death situations. You don't have to almost die for those instincts to be triggered. They are for every situation.

Take sexuality, for example. It's no secret that some of the most successful advertisements are the ones that include images of sexy ladies. Why is that?

Because it's a primitive instinct, and to be frank, it influences men to make impulsive monetary decisions.

Psychology Tip:

Researchers have found that men viewing girls in bikinis make impulsive (and worse) decisions when it comes to money.[5] In an experiment, men were offered an immediate sum of $25 or the option to negotiate for a larger amount after a time, such as a week or a month later. Those who viewed the sexier images demanded only $7 extra for waiting a month, while those who didn't view sexy images demanded double that amount.

2] The Midbrain (Mammalian)

The midbrain is all about your state of mind, your emotions—the part that people think is best to be in control of.

I've got news for you. People are never in control of this part of the brain either, even if they think they are.

How often have you made impulse purchases and thought to yourself, *"What was I thinking when I bought that?"*

It was a gut feeling, and you went with it. It's that simple.

Or is it?

Our midbrain actually makes decisions based on **emotions, value judgments,** and **the reward** for making those decisions.

1. **Emotions** are how we feel. Are you joyful? Sad? Stressed?
2. **A value judgment** is not necessarily the right judgment, but it's the judgment you make based on your gut feeling at that point in time. For example, you just met someone new; you have a "feeling" about that person. Maybe you like him, or perhaps you don't. Either way, you don't have the rationale to judge this person based on this one encounter, but it's still happening in the back of your mind without you even thinking about it. Maybe the way he shook your hand was not firm enough, which makes you dislike him. It could be his outfit or his voice. Maybe it's his haircut. Perhaps it's just the energy he brings.
3. **Rewards** are what boost dopamine in your body. It's the "feel-good" hormone, the "well done" cheer. You eat chocolate and you feel pleasure, so you grab another bite ... and another bite. You don't really think of the calories or how much weight you will gain when you eat a gigantic chocolate bar. And later you think, *"WHAT WAS I THINKING?"*

This is the reason you make impulsive purchases. It's because of that "feel-good," "well done" reward feeling you get when buying the product.

Imagine you are sitting on your couch in your living room scrolling through your phone while watching Netflix. You saw an ad, clicked on it, and landed on a beautiful, professional-looking website, selling a product that will solve one of your biggest issues at work and save you tons of time. You don't think twice; you make a "value judgment," click "Add to Cart," and enter your credit card details. Finally, the package arrives, and you feel good, *or* maybe you regret it and think, *"What was I thinking?"*

One more stupid thing you just did. But here is the good news: it's not always stupid.

In fact, if we don't make "value judgments," we would be paralyzed and stumble over every decision we need to make.

We are wired to use our emotions, value judgments, and energy to increase that dopamine in our system.

We strive for a "well done."

The New Brain (Neocortex)

This is the logical part of your brain. The pros and cons list I created with all the carefully laid out weights and satisfaction percentages was the new brain trying to convince me I was making the right decision. You need this logical bit to rationalize your decision AFTER you have made it. In my case, my logical analysis didn't support my decision. That rationalization from my "new brain" was missing, which left me with doubt, second-guessing my decision, and more often than not, regretting the decision because my carefully crafted logical model did not support it.

Here is something to keep in mind.

Even though the logical part does very little in your decision-making process, it is what will justify your decision again and again.

We all know that salads are more expensive than fast food. Despite this, many people choose a salad as their lunch choice over fast food. Why is this? Well, they rationalize that they are choosing to be healthy. Even though they are paying more now, they are saving tons of money on doctors and hospitals as a result of eating too much junk food.

Once the decision is made, it becomes easier to justify it. There is an argument for any side of the story; you just have to put it together and make sure your customer is aware of it. *(More in Chapter 9: Do They Know about It?)*

Consumers' Motivations: *Why do your customers need to do the jobs they want to get done?*

Our three brains trigger our buying decisions, but our buying decisions are fueled by our desires.

What is desire?

Desire is the wants, needs, and cravings that drive your customer through life. It could be **physical,** such as the desire to have smooth skin or a toned physique. It could be **material,** such as the desire to live in an expensive neighborhood or own a fancy car. It could also be **sensual,** such as the desire to take a hot shower or walk into an air-conditioned room after having been sweating in the summer sun.

When you understand your customers' desires, you will be able to answer the question *"What's in it for me?"* By answering this question, you will get your customers' attention.

There are eight foundational desires that shape our wants and needs and speak to our biological triggers. In his book *Ca$hvertising*, Drew Eric Whitman calls them the Life-Force 8 (LF8 for short).[6] If you use a few of these needs, or even just one, you will be speaking right to your customers. You will answer the question, *"What's in it for me?"* That's what usually makes us make decisions. We want to know what's in it for us.

So, what are the eight foundational desires?

1. Survival, enjoyment of life, life extension
2. Enjoyment of food and beverages
3. Freedom from fear, pain, and danger
4. Sexual companionship
5. Comfortable living conditions
6. To be superior, winning, keeping up with the Joneses
7. Care and protection of loved ones
8. Social approval

"When you create an advertising appeal based on any of the LF8, you tap into the power of Mother Nature herself. You tap into the very essence of what makes humans tick. You see, you can't escape your desires for the LF8. You were born with them, and they'll be with you until the day you die." -Drew Eric Whitman, Ca$hvertising [7]

These eight biological triggers first speak to our old and midbrain and then our new brain. We want to survive and enjoy life. That's why most people stayed at home during the COVID-19 pandemic; they wanted to stay home to stay safe, which not only hit on the survival trigger (#1) but also freedom from fear, pain, and danger (#3).

It's no wonder people went to the supermarket and started buying groceries like maniacs and making panic purchases. This was because of survival (trigger #1); the food and beverages trigger (#2); freedom from fear, pain, and danger (#3); the desire for

comfortable living conditions (trigger #5); and the need to care
and protection of loved ones (trigger #7).

Entire cities ran out of toilet paper.

One action, one decision, one purchase could be triggered not
only by one biological trigger but a combination of the eight life
forces.

Maslow's Hierarchy of Needs

If you think about it, the eight biological triggers are in sync with
Maslow's Hierarchy of Needs.

Maslow's Hierarchy of Needs is a psychological motivational
model with five levels of needs depicted as a pyramid. Needs at
the bottom levels must first be satisfied (or somewhat satisfied)
before individuals tend to the higher levels.

*"It is quite true that man lives by bread alone - when
there is no bread. But what happens to man's desires
when there is plenty of bread and when his belly is
chronically filled? At once other (and "higher") needs
emerge, these, rather than physiological hungers,
dominate the organism. And when these, in turn, are
satisfied, again, new (and still "higher") needs emerge, and
so on. This is what we mean by saying that the basic
human needs are organized into a hierarchy of relative
prepotency." -A. H. Maslow[8]*

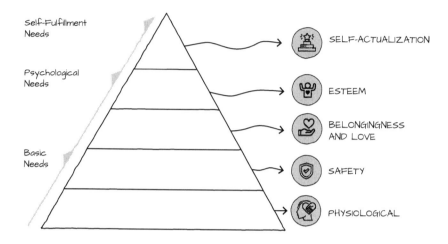

Source: Maslow's Hierarchy of Needs

Starting from the bottom of the hierarchy, the needs are as follows:[9]

1. **Physiological** needs are the basic biological requirements for human survival. *Examples: Air, water, food, shelter, sleep, clothing, warmth, and sex.*

2. **Safety** refers to the need to feel secure and safe. People want to experience order, predictability, and control in their lives. These needs can be fulfilled by the family and society (e.g., police, schools, business, and medical care). *Examples: Personal security, employment, business, resources, property, police, schools, and medical care.*

3. **Love and belonging** refer to a human emotional need for interpersonal relationships, affiliating, connectedness, and being part of a group. *Examples: Friendship, intimate relationships, family, sense of connection, trust, acceptance, affection, and love.*

4. **Esteem** refers to 1] Esteem for oneself. *Examples include dignity, achievement, mastery, independence, freedom, strength, and feeling of accomplishment.* 2] Desire for

reputation or respect from others. *Examples: Status, prestige, and recognition. Maslow indicated that the desire for reputation and respect from others is more important for children and adolescents than self-esteem.*

5. **Self-actualization** needs pertain to achieving one's full potential and becoming the most one can be. Needs in self-fulfillment and personal growth vary from one person to another depending on what is important to them. *Examples: Becoming an ideal parent, expressing creativity through paintings, pictures, or invention, or realizing economic, academic, or athletic achievements.*

Each individual's priorities are different. For example, some people may value self-esteem over love—or love over safety.

Needs do not have to be 100% fulfilled to move to the next level of the pyramid, and one's motivation is not necessarily driven by just one need. It could be a mixture of needs. For example, someone buying a house in a safe and prestigious neighborhood to start a family is a decision based on four needs:

1. **Physiological needs:** Shelter, water, electricity, internet, etc.
2. **Safety needs:** Safe neighborhood.
3. **Love and belonging:** Starting a family to belong to.
4. **Esteem:** The prestigious neighborhood will associate the person with a specific status and earn the respect of their social circle.

"Any behavior tends to be determined by several or all of the basic needs simultaneously rather than by only one of them." -Maslow[10]

The Expanded Hierarchy of Needs[11]

The hierarchy of needs has been expanded to include cognitive, aesthetic (Maslow, 1970a), and transcendence needs (Maslow, 1970b).

1. **Physiological Needs**: Original
2. **Safety Needs**: Original
3. **Love and Belonging**: Original
4. **Esteem**: Original
5. **Cognitive Needs**: The need for meaning, predictability, knowledge, understanding, curiosity, and exploration.
6. **Aesthetic Needs**: The search for beauty, balance, form, and appreciation.
7. **Self-Actualization**: Original
8. **Transcendence Needs**: The values that motivate a person which transcend beyond the personal self. *Examples: Mystical experiences and certain experiences with nature, aesthetic experiences, sexual experiences, service to others, the pursuit of science, religious faith, etc.*

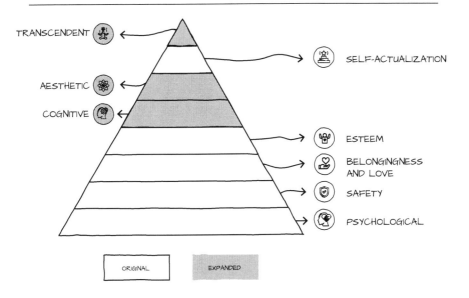

Source: Maslow's Expanded Hierarchy of Needs

Deficiency Needs vs. Growth Needs

The first four levels (starting from the bottom) are referred to as deficiency needs, including your basic and physiological needs, which means they arrive due to deprivation. When they are not met, the motivation to fulfill them arises. On the top (in addition to the expanded cognitive, aesthetic, and transcendence needs), the fifth level is referred are the growth needs, which means they can only be fulfilled if the other needs are met.

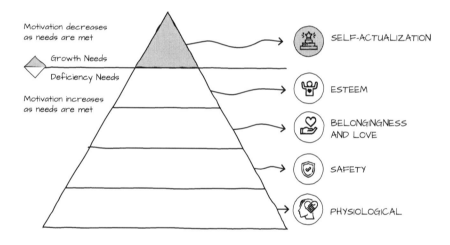

Deficiency Needs vs. Growth Needs

You might have noticed that the eight biological triggers line up with the first four levels.

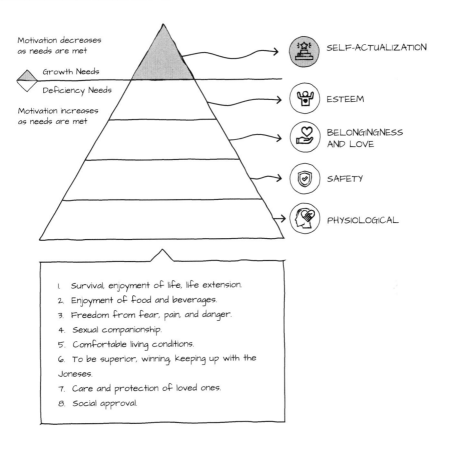

1. Survival, enjoyment of life, life extension.
2. Enjoyment of food and beverages.
3. Freedom from fear, pain, and danger.
4. Sexual companionship.
5. Comfortable living conditions.
6. To be superior, winning, keeping up with the Joneses.
7. Care and protection of loved ones.
8. Social approval.

The Hierarchy of Needs and the Eight Biological Triggers

The 5 Whys Technique: *How do you know which biological triggers captivate your customers?*

You might be thinking, *"This all sounds great, but when it comes to my product, how do I know which biological triggers captivate my customers?"*

Identify a need (or a job to be done) and trace it back to one of these eight needs, or perhaps a combination of them.

How do you determine which needs and wants are associated with your products or services?

This is where the **5 Whys Technique** comes in handy.

The 5 Whys Technique: What is it?

It is originally a root-cause analysis technique used to solve problems, developed by Sakichi Toyoda,[12] the Japanese industrialist, inventor, and founder of Toyota Industries in the 1930s. It became popular in the 1970s, and Toyota still uses it to solve problems today.

The 5 Whys Technique is used to solve problems, troubleshoot issues, and improve the quality of your products.

And we can use it to identify the motivations and the true desires of our customers.

How to use the 5 Whys to uncover your customers' motivations and desires:

You can either brainstorm with your team (those who have been working with customers day in, day out), or you can have a chat with a few of your customers. It's always better to speak to the customers because no matter how much you want to wear your customers' "hat," you may still miss out on a few things here and there and end up with some blindspots.

First, determine which job you want to understand the desires and motivations of. *(Refer to Chapter 2: What Do They Want to Do?)*

Then, ask the first why.

Asking "why" is simple, but simple doesn't mean there is no serious thought behind it. You want to truly understand "why."

Then, ask the remaining four "whys."

Try to avoid coming to any conclusions until you get the answer to your 5th and final why. How do you do this? Ask them right after the other. Don't dwell on one for too long.

There are, however, times you might not need all five whys, which depends on the job at hand.

Last year in 2020, when COVID-19 hit and I was stuck in my small studio apartment, I decided to move. It was time for me to find my new home, and so the job I had to do was to *"move to a new apartment."*

Job: I want to move to a new apartment.

WHY 1:

Why do you want to move?

Because I am not feeling comfortable in the apartment I am living in now.

WHY 2:

Why don't you feel comfortable?

Because ...

1. I feel like I am suffocating because there is very limited space. **There is no room to do anything.**
2. I also want to have a balcony. I don't even have a window that opens. **I need fresh air!**

Did you notice that the second why had two answers? This magic method has the fascinating ability to uncover more desires, more motivations.

WHY 3:

Why do you need space? And fresh air?

1. I want to be able to be creative, have whiteboards on the walls, paint, and write. **I want to unlock my creativity and have a fresh mind.**
2. I want to exercise at home as well and have a space to paint!

WHY 4:

Why do you want to unlock your creativity?

1. I want to unlock my creativity because I am working on my first book, which I have been dreaming about writing for years.
2. I also want to start painting again in my free time.

Why do you want to exercise?

1. I want to exercise because I am starting to gain weight, and I want to be fit.

WHY 5:

Why do you want to write a book?

1. It has been a personal goal for about ten years. I have knowledge that I want to share. I have been researching and gaining many

insights about consumer behavior (one of my many passions), and I want to share it with everyone who can benefit from it.

Why do you want to start painting again in your free time?

1. I want to start painting again in my free time because it makes me less stressed. I release my negative energy and express my deepest fears and frustrations, creating something beautiful in the process.

Why do you want to be fit?

1. Because I want to look good in my clothes and look hot. Doesn't everyone?

The following Mind Map illustrates how we arrived at these desires.

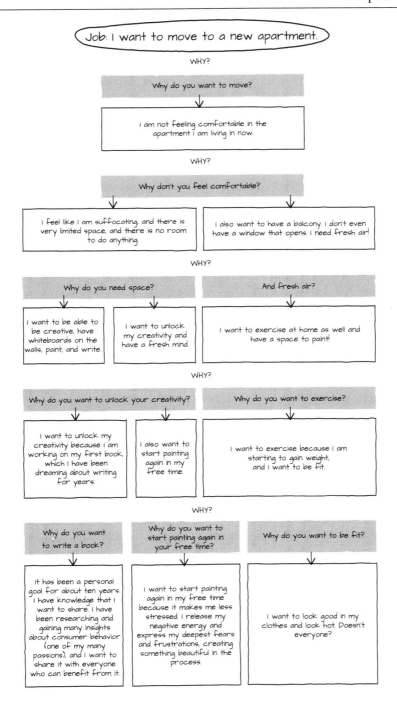

The 5 Whys Technique Mind Map

You see, the more you ask why, the more you uncover deep, hidden desires, which on the surface, seem like they have nothing to do with "moving to a new apartment." Trust in the process, and you will uncover far more exciting insights than you could have possibly imagined.

After you ask the first five whys, start tracing each motivation and desire back to the eight biological triggers.

Here you will find exciting outcomes. You want to see which biological triggers are associated with all the jobs your customers do. You might see a trend, which could be one of the most important keys to effective campaigns, copywriting, and advertisements. *(Refer to Chapter 9: Do They Know about It?)*

Tip:

Continue asking why if you feel there could be more motivations to uncover. No one is stopping you. ☺

Dimensions of Desire and Its Strength: *Is it worth it for your business to pursue those desires?*

Asking the five whys will help you identify the different desires that your customers have. The desires associated with each job are just as important as knowing the jobs your customers want to do. It's equally important to know the strength of those desires.

There are three dimensions of desire, mentioned by Eugene M. Schwartz in his book *Breakthrough Advertising*.[13]

1. **Urgency, intensity, and degree of demand to be satisfied.** *How often do you get that urge?* Think constant migraine vs. minor headache.

2. **Staying power, degree of repetition, and the inability to be satiated.** *How badly do your customers want that desire to be satisfied?* Think raw hunger vs. craving a gourmet meal.

3. **Scope, the number of people who share this desire.** *How many people have this desire?* Think the number of people who would buy a quality durable product vs. those who don't mind paying for repairs or buying a new version every now and then.

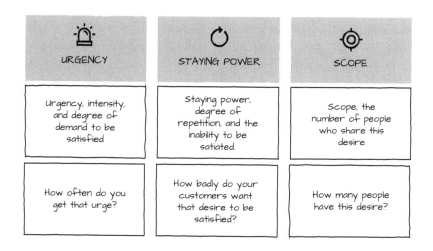

The Three Dimensions of Desire

For each of the desires you identify in your customer, you want to understand which of the three dimensions it is. Simply put, the desire answers the question, *"What's in it for me?"* for your customer. The dimensions answer the question, *"Is it worth it for me?"* for your business. In other words, is it worth it for your business to pursue that desire?

You can analyze any customer desire based on these three dimensions.

For example, if your customer desires to **enjoy great homemade food**, what is the strength of this desire from 1 to 10 for each of those dimensions?

1. Urgency, intensity, and degree of demand to be satisfied:
   - Customer: *I have wanted to eat homemade food every day since COVID-19. It makes me feel safe.*

2. Staying power, degree of repetition, and the inability to be satiated:
    * Customer: *I need to eat at least 2-3 times a day.*
3. Scope, the number of people who share this desire:
    * Customer: *Let's say hypothetically, 70% of the population of Dubai prefer homemade food over delivery post the COVID-19 period.*

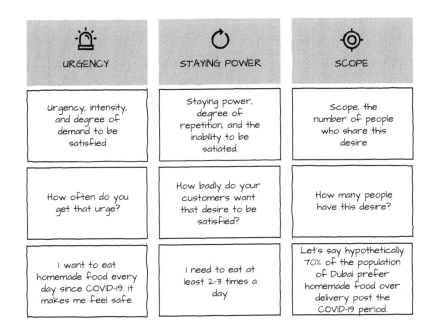

The Three Dimensions of Desire

If we take one of the desires we unlocked in the five whys exercise, we can still apply the same thinking. For example, the desire is: **I want to look good in my clothes and look hot.**

1. Urgency, intensity, and degree of demand to be satisfied:
    * Customer: *I want to look good every day when I go to work or meet my friends.*

2. Staying power, degree of repetition, and the inability to be satiated:
   - Customer: *I go out to work every day and see my friends pretty often.*
3. Scope, the number of people who share this desire:
   - Customer: *Let's say, hypothetically, 60% of the female population of Dubai have full-time jobs.*

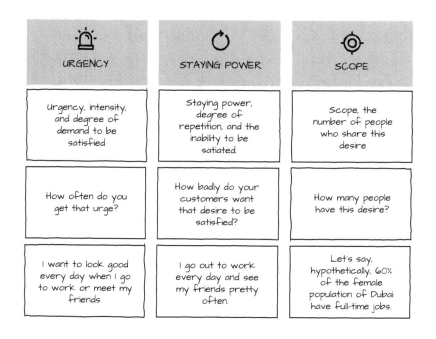

The Three Dimensions of Desire

What happens if your customer doesn't achieve their goal?

You should now understand the jobs your customer wants to do and the desires and motivations behind them.

Still, how important is it to know the jobs and desires of our customers if we don't know what happens when their desire isn't fulfilled?

For example, let's say my core job is to grow my hair, and the desire associated with that core job is to feel attractive and confident. What happens if I don't grow my hair?

Practically speaking, that was me my whole life, but I just embraced having short hair and had fun with it. In that case, growing my hair is, yes, a job I want to do, and my desire to feel attractive and confident is something I still want to have. Perhaps, I can even feel beautiful and confident without that long hair. That desire is not a pressing issue for me.

On the other hand, if we think about the COVID-19 quarantine situation, everyone panicked and bought loads of groceries from the supermarket when lockdown was first announced. Shoppers were buying canned goods and as many non-perishable goods as they could carry. The desire was clear. It was survival. It was protecting and taking care of loved ones. It was making sure you were living in comfortable conditions. What would happen if you didn't prepare? You might starve. You might not have food to feed your kids. Primitive instincts kicked in.

Psychology Tip:

Loss aversion was first identified by Nobel Prize Winner Daniel Kahneman[14] in 1984. It is a psychological principle that says we are more motivated when we are about to lose something than when we are about to gain something new. As a result, people will go to great lengths to avoid losing, stating that the psychological pain of losing is twice as powerful as the pleasure of winning.

Chapter Quiz

So, you've made it to the end of Chapter 3. You have learned all about your customers' needs, desires, and biological triggers. Great job finishing this chapter!

Think you're ready for the chapter quiz?

True/False

1: You make decisions rationally first, and then check if it's in sync with your gut feeling. (True/False)

2: When choosing a customer desire to address, it's best to evaluate its intensity, staying power, and the number of people who have this desire before building your product around it. (True/False)

Quiz Answer Key

Answer 1: False. 95% of your decisions are made in the subconscious mind. First, you decide using your gut feeling; then, you look for rational evidence to support that decision.

Answer 2: True. Customer desires answer the question *"What's in it for me?"* for your customers, but understanding the three dimensions of that desire will determine if it's even worth it for your business to go with that desire. It has to be a pressing desire that a significant amount of people have.

Putting It All into Action

You've gained so much insight about desires and biological triggers, and if you want to uncover them for your customers, it's time to buckle up and unwrap those thoughts to put them all into action.

Here's your checklist:

1. Identify the jobs your customers do.
2. Identify which jobs you would like to look into.
3. Ask the five whys to uncover your customers' hidden desires and motivations.
4. Map your customers' hidden desires and motivations to the eight biological needs.
5. Identify the three dimensions of desire and the strength of each desire:
   - Urgency, intensity, and degree of demand to be satisfied
   - Staying power, degree of repetition, and the inability to be satiated
   - Scope, the number of people who share this desire
6. Identify what happens if your customer doesn't achieve that desire.

You're well on your way to understanding your customers' hidden desires and motivations, so now it's time to move on to Chapter 4 to find out what is stopping them from buying your product.

References

1. Theodore Levitt. "'People Don't Want to Buy a Quarter-Inch Drill. They Want a QUARTER-INCH HOLE!,'" n.d. https://blogs.ubc.ca/marvinamm/2011/09/26/people-dont-want-to-buy-a-quarter-inch-drill-they-want-a-quarter-inch-hole/.
2. Gerald Zaltman. "Hidden Minds." Harvard Business Review, August 1, 2014. https://hbr.org/2002/06/hidden-minds.
3. Roger Dooley. "Brainfluence." Roger Dooley, July 22, 2021. https://www.rogerdooley.com/books/brainfluence/.
4. Seth Godin. "Fight Your Lizard Brain." The Imperfectionist, March 28, 2015. https://imperfectionistblog.com/2015/03/fight-your-lizard-brain/.
5. Dooley, "Brainfluence," 2015.
6. Drew Eric Whitman. "Cashvertising: How to Use More Than 100 Secrets Of Ad-Agency Psychology to Make Big Money Selling Anything to Anyone." Drew Eric Whitman, 2009. https://drewericwhitman.com/products/.
7. Whitman, "Cashvertising," 2009.
8. A. H. Maslow. "A Theory of Human Motivation." Psychological Review 50, no. 4 (1943): 370–96. https://doi.org/10.1037/h0054346.
9. Maslow, "Theory of Human Motivation," 1943.
10. Maslow, "Theory of Human Motivation," 1943.
11. Saul Mcleod. "Maslow's Hierarchy of Needs." Simply Psychology, December 29, 2020. https://www.simplypsychology.org/maslow.html.

12. Toyota Industries Corporation Copyright © Toyota Industries Corporation. All rights reserved. "The Story of Sakichi Toyoda." The Story of Sakichi Toyoda | Toyota Industries Corporation. Accessed 2021. https://www.toyota-industries.com/company/history/toyoda_sakichi/.

13. Eugene Schwartz, and Edelston, Martin. "Breakthrough Advertising ." Breakthrough Advertising. Brian Kurtz, 2017. https://breakthroughadvertisingbook.com/.

14. Daniel Kahneman, Knetsch, Jack L, and Thaler, Richard H. "Anomalies: The Endowment Effect, Loss Aversion, and Status Quo Bias." Journal of Economic Perspectives 5, no. 1 (1991): 193–206. https://doi.org/10.1257/jep.5.1.193.

CHAPTER 4

What Is Stopping Them?

"Walking a mile in someone else's shoes isn't as much about the walk or the shoes; it's to be able to think like they think, feel what they feel, and understand why they are who and where they are. Every step is about empathy."

—Toni Sorenson[1]

Chapter Objectives:

- **Behavioral Change:** What motivates action and behavioral change?
- **Customer Challenges:** How do you find out your customer's challenges?
- **Customer Segmentation:** How do you segment your customers?
- **Customer Journey:** How do you understand your customer's journey?
- **Mystery Shopping:** How do you validate your understanding of the customer journey?

When I was ten years old, I had a Boxer named Rocky. I was absolutely in love with him. I loved to play with him. When he was still a puppy, he would sleep with me on my bed. His eyes expressed nothing but love. The way his tail wagged when he saw me made coming home to see him my biggest reward.

I loved feeding him and spending time with him—that is, until I realized I didn't know what to do about him pooping everywhere. I didn't know much about dogs at the time, let alone how to take care of them.

So it went, until one summer, my brother and I went on a trip. When we came back, Rocky was gone.

While we were gone, my mom had decided she was fed up with the whole mess. She had given him away to someone who could train and take care of him properly.

I was so sad and disheartened. I missed him so much. He came to visit from time to time, and each time he did, his little tail danced as his soft eyes met mine. He would run around, sniffing through my things and giving me hugs and kisses.

Rocky was so dear to me that I couldn't help it when, in 2021, after the lockdown and going through a hard time alone, I thought maybe it was time to adopt a dog. Rocky would always lift my spirits. He would light up the room, and he would always make guests feel loved. I wanted to experience that joy again. I wanted to have a living creature in my apartment to interact with and make me feel less lonely. So I thought about it, and I even checked out a few places where I could adopt a dog—but then I remembered the poop.

I thought,

- *Oh my God! There will be poop everywhere.*
- *I have to have the proper dog training so that I can handle a new dog.*
- *I would have to walk it twice a day.*
- *I travel all the time for work. Who will feed and walk him while I'm gone?*
- *Dubai summers are too harsh and humid to be walking a dog. Just last week it was so hot, it felt like it was probably 50+ degrees Celsius (122 degrees Fahrenheit)! The poor thing would suffer—and so would I!*

All those thoughts came to mind, and suddenly the idea of getting a dog didn't seem like such a good idea.

I discussed it with my best friend, and she suggested something I hadn't previously considered.

"If you aren't ready for a dog, how about a cat? They are very low maintenance creatures. You don't need to walk them. I could even check up on your kitty while you're traveling."

I thought, *Hmmm ... That doesn't sound like such a bad idea.*

My best friend and I went to check out cats together, only to find that I was more drawn to the dogs in the pet shop.

Part of me wanted to get a dog, not a cat. Still, the cats were so adorable. I didn't know there were such cute cat breeds ... For the life of me, I couldn't decide.

So, I didn't end up with a dog or a cat.

Guess what I ended up with.

Plants.

Plants bring life to a home.

I thought cats were low maintenance, but plants are even better in that department! I took care of mine by simply giving them a splash of water every now and then. Sure, they don't snuggle, and they don't look at me with kind, loving eyes. They don't wag their tail, and they certainly don't jump around. There is no way for them to show me they love me.

But they did make my apartment more homey.

Using my dog story, here is a brief analysis of the topics we discussed in the previous chapters:

- **Job**: The job I wanted to get done was to have a pet that would lift my spirits and light up the room.
- **Competition**: The dog's competition was a cat and plants. I ended up with the plants.
- **Desire**: I wanted a lively home with a pet to take care of so I wouldn't feel so alone.

I had a desire to fulfill. I wanted a home that was full of life. I wanted to ease my loneliness, so I wanted a pet. I wanted to get a dog specifically, but many things stopped me from doing so; it would have been more work than I was ready for.

I spoke again with my best friend, and since I still was considering getting a dog, she suggested I hire a dog walker. *"You don't have to do it yourself,"* she said. Then she added, *"There are dog training schools that could train your dog as well."*

While these were all reasonable solutions, something still stopped me. I felt scared of the responsibility, and I didn't want to let my dog down. I wanted my dog to be well taken care of.

So, with that in mind, and now that you know who your customer is, remember Sally from Chapter 1? Do you know what is stopping her? What's getting in her way?

Behavioral Change: *What motivates action and behavioral change?*

The purpose of your product or service is to replace another product or service your customer is currently using to get a job done. And the competition could be something that might never have occurred to you.

Remember the milkshake story? *(Refer to Chapter 2: What Do They Want to Do?)*

You are competing with the many distractions your customers have. Customers have many options and limited time on their hands, so you want to convert them by taking them away from what they do now that isn't working to what you want them to do that will make their lives easier.

Simply put, your customers don't have enough time to do all the things they want to do.

Zumba classes compete with the gym. Gluten-free, lactose-free, sugar-free muffins are competing with the classic muffin. Uber is competing with a taxi. Airbnb is competing with hotels. Instagram stories are competing with Snapchat. And even Netflix announced that TikTok is its major competition.

Hey, how can you convert customers from using what they use now to using your product or service instead?

We are talking here about behavioral change. You might be thinking something along the lines of:

- No one can change anyone.
- Change happens only from within.

I have good news. Behavioral change is possible, and there is a formula for it.

Motivation + Ease = Behavioral Change

When you want to do anything, two components make it happen:
1. Motivation
2. Ease

How do motivation and ease relate to behavioral change?

Well, let's start with some simple definitions.

1] Motivation

Motivation is triggered by two things, as mentioned in the book, *The Advertising Effect: How to Change Behaviour* by Adam Ferrier and Jennifer Fleming.[2]

A] Individual Incentives: People are motivated to either seek pleasure or avoid pain.

For example, it's much easier to convince someone to get the business lunch deal if they are already hungry, whereas if they aren't, it might not be so easy.

Look to the eight basic needs and wants that trigger our behavioral desires to break down the possible incentives. *(Refer to Chapter 3: Why Do They Want to Do It?)*

B] Social Norms: People seek to know if this behavior is accepted by the social community they are in. It's pretty common to see people scared to speak up or try something different just to avoid the judgment of being an outlier. They want to fit in and be accepted. They want to follow social norms.

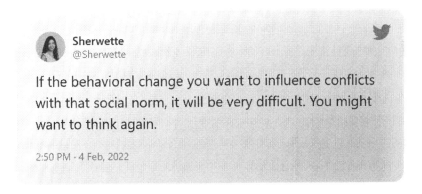

Sherwette
@Sherwette

If the behavioral change you want to influence conflicts with that social norm, it will be very difficult. You might want to think again.

2:50 PM · 4 Feb, 2022

Psychology Tip:

> Watching what others do has a far greater impact on our behavior than internal motivations, according to psychologist Albert Bandura (1977). Humans strive to be perceived as part of the social norm. Fishbein and Ajzen (1975) are two psychologists studying this specific topic. They articulate that social norms significantly influence someone's decisions, especially when it comes to other people's perceptions of who is important to that person. Do those important people think it's a behavior that she should or should not do? The answer to that question greatly impacts human behavior.[3]

2] Ease

Ease is also defined by two main factors.

A] Ability: Is that person actually capable of doing this task? Does she have the skills to do it?

B] Opportunity: Is the person placed in an environment that allows this to happen? Was she able to see that the restaurant had a business lunch offer when passing it by? Does she have enough time to dine in, or does he have to rush off to a meeting she is late for?

Behavioral Change Based on Motivation and Ease

We have spoken plenty about motivation in Chapter 3 *(Why Do They Want to Do It?)*, so while motivation through desire is very important, the ease of doing things is just as important.

In fact, if someone wants to change their behavior altogether, motivation alone is not enough. That's why so many people revert back to their old eating habits after starting to diet for a few days, weeks, or even months.

Motivation, however, when coupled with ease, produces behavioral change.

When your customer wants to do something, but it's not easy for them to do it, they stop trying. This is where challenges come into play.

For example, if I want to make barista coffee at home, but it takes ten minutes to prepare my coffee machine every morning, I will skip it and perhaps have instant coffee instead to be ready to go.

I do prefer to enjoy my food and beverages *(biological trigger #2, see Chapter 3: Why Do They Want to Do It?)*, but not at the expense of time when it's very limited.

Here, my challenge is time. Others might have different challenges, such as not having access to great coffee beans or not knowing how to brew beans at home.

In his book *The Advertising Effect,*[4] Adam Ferrier uses the following grid to show the four areas of behavioral framing based on motivation and ease:

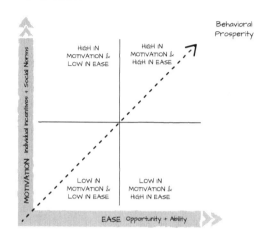

Source: The Advertising Effect by Adam Ferrier

1] Behaviors high in motivation and high in ease - *Example: A person is hungry and there is a chocolate bar in front of him.*

2] Behaviors high in motivation but low in ease - *Example: A person is hungry and has to go to the store to buy food.*

3] Behaviors low in motivation but high in ease - *Example: Offering a person who is not hungry a chocolate bar.*

4] Behaviors low in motivation and low in ease - *Example: Asking someone who is not hungry to go to the store to buy food.*

This grid will help you know what component of the behavioral change to focus on. To do so, use the following questions as a diagnostic tool to pinpoint barriers to behavioral change.

Motivation Questions:

A - Individual Incentives: What's in it for them? What's their reward? And how big is it?

B - Social Norms: What would other people they care about think when they do that specific behavior?

Ease Questions:

A- Ability: Can they do it? Are they equipped with the right resources, competencies, and skills to undertake this behavior?

B- Opportunity: Do the circumstances and surrounding environment make it easy and encourage this behavior to happen?

Customer Challenges: *How do you find out your customer's challenges?*

How do you find out your
customer's challenges?

You ask.

Please don't fall into the trap that many "experts" fall into. The following phrases are said more often than you think ...

- *"We know our customers' challenges."*
- *"Our customer challenges are x, y, and z."*
- *"We hired consultants in the industry who know our customer's challenges even better than our customers."*
- *"We don't need to ask our customers because we know what is best for them. They don't know what they want."*
- *"We are consultants. We know best. That's why the client hired us."*

Does any of the above sound familiar?

Personally, I know I've heard it time and time again as part of my job, whether it came from clients themselves or even my fellow consultants.

I hate to kill the buzz.

But "knowing best" won't get you anywhere.

Customer research is one of the tasks many people dread, but it's an absolute must, to say the least.

When you speak to your customers, you get closer to them and understand them better, getting to know their desires and their struggles in order to serve them better.

It doesn't have to be complicated. You don't need extensive amounts of research to learn about your customers' challenges. There are tons of methods you can apply, whether they are qualitative or quantitative, and you don't have to do all of them to understand your customers. *(Refer to Chapter 1: Who Do You Want to Serve?)*

To understand what is stopping your customers from doing what they want to do, all you need to do is ... *ask*.

Here's one of my favorite research methods introduced by Ryan Levesque, which is called the Ask Method (https://askmethod. com/).[5] It's simple and effective.

Whether you want to conduct a survey, have a one-on-one interview, a focus group, or just scan the internet for forums where your customers are complaining—it doesn't matter. All that matters is that you ask. Ryan recommends the ones that are more personal and involve the customer by conducting a survey or by asking one-on-one in online conversations with your target market. His rationale is that when people write their challenges and you play those challenges back to them in marketing campaigns, they will feel as if you are reading their minds.

Ryan's method comes down to what he calls the **Single Most Important Question (SMIQ).**

SMIQ: *"So, when it comes to X, what is the single biggest challenge or frustration right now? Please be as detailed and specific as possible."*

It's just that simple yet incredibly effective.

You ask, and then all you have to do is listen. Listen to every word.

Tip:

Follow-up with a 1:1 interview after the survey to uncover more insights. Remember, you want to do as little talking as possible. This interview is for you to hear from your customers and understand them better.

Try to prompt your customers to express more of their challenges. The more they do, the more you understand what is stopping them, and the better you'll be able to serve them.

I encourage you to read *Ask* by Ryan Levesque to learn more about the Ask Method. There is science behind it, and the way he lays it out will make a few light bulbs go off in your head.

But then, what should you do with that repository of challenges?

Customer Segmentation: *How do you segment your customers?*

More often than not, I see a common practice of segmenting customers by their demographics or binary descriptions. It's a good start but a massive fallback if that is your only segmentation. If you segment your customers based on demographics data alone, you miss out on the mere essence of all the work you have been doing so far.

We are all different, yet we are all the same.

We are the same because we share similar desires, and in having those desires, we face similar challenges. We are the same when it comes to tackling certain jobs or trying to get over a specific challenge.

If you want to make a barista coffee at home, it doesn't matter if you are a man or a woman. Your age doesn't matter. What really matters is if you truly enjoy coffee. What matters is if it's essential to your routine. What matters is how much time you have to prepare it at home, how often you go grocery shopping, and whether or not you enjoy or dread cleaning kitchen supplies. Would you say that you are fussy about coffee? Do you savor it or just shoot back some espresso and call it a day?

This is where it's crucial to segment the customers first based on their jobs-to-be-done, and second, based on the challenges they face trying to get those jobs done. Only then will you be able to serve them based on those challenges, help them do the job faster and better, and communicate with them in a language they understand.

When you segment your customers based on their challenges, you will be able to bucket them according to their struggles, which will help you in many ways.

First, you will notice which challenges are worth pursuing. Because if a challenge exists, but it isn't paining very many of your customers, you might as well not invest your time and effort into trying to resolve this challenge.

Secondly, segmenting customers based on their challenges will allow you to cater your products to those challenges.

Third, you will write your copy and talk to your customers to resolve those challenges. You are not selling your brand. You are selling a solution to your customers' most pressing issues.

Customer Journey: *How do you understand your customer's journey?*

To connect with your customer, you want to understand her story. In Chapter One *(Who Do You Want to Serve?)*, you created your perfect person, your persona. You identified her, you stalked her on social media, and up until this chapter, you understood so much about her, including what she wants to do and why she wants to do it. By now, you should also know what is stopping her and the challenges she faces while trying to do the things she wants to do.

So, here is a question to think about ... **Where do those challenges lie in your customer's journey?**

First, what is a customer journey?

A **Journey Map** shows your customer's experiences over time. It could be applied to a physical or digital product, a service, or brand. The Journey Map represents the different events in which your customer interacted with your brand, including recognizing a need they have, searching for the solution, finding the product or service that fulfills it, paying for it, using it, complaining about it, and recommending it to a friend.

Customer journeys uncover much more than think.

It is one of my very favorite methods when conducting research and understanding my customers. Mapping your customer's journey helps you understand your customer's experience, where her motivations lie—what makes her start, stumble, stop, or keep going.

That said, how do you start mapping your customer's journey?

There are a few things to keep in mind when it comes to mapping your customer's journey. The following are referred to as lanes:

1. **The Main Actor, Your Persona:** Your persona, for example, Sally, represents a segment of your customers, and she gives life to the story. You may need to create more than one customer journey based on the different personas you serve in your business.

2. **Journey Stages:** Stages compile a group of customer steps, representing a high-level phase of the customer journey. For example, need identification, information search, product comparison, product selection and purchase, usage, and maintenance. It can also be as simple as before buying, during buying, and after buying.

3. **Journey Steps:** Steps are any interactions that your persona, Sally, has with your brand or your competition. It could be any activity she takes on her own, such as walking or driving. It's all the experiences she goes through to finally reach and use your product or service. What does Sally do from the moment she even thinks about her problem or trigger that could lead

to your product, all the way up to buying it and recommending it to her friends? What initiates or agitates her desires? What does she do to search for information? How does she choose to communicate with others? How does she usually pay for services? And what does she do if she is fed up with your service and decides to file a complaint? Does she post on social media? Steps are a few words that describe the interaction.

4. **Story:** This is where the narrative should be. While journey stages and steps give you an even closer look at what Sally experiences, the narrative of her story will make you think of the details that influence all her senses. You will be able to imagine and really get in touch with her and walk in her shoes to understand the pleasure or pain of her experience.

5. **Touchpoints:** While journey steps describe every step your customer goes through, touchpoints are specific moments when the customer interacts with your brand before, during, or after making a purchase. During which steps in Sally's journey does she interact with YOU (or you in the future) or YOUR competition?

6. **Moments of Truth:** These are the moments that either make or break the relationship your Sally has with your brand. Moments of truth are nonnegotiable. For example, if you go to a restaurant and the host who took you to your table didn't welcome you with a flashing smile on her face, that's not a big deal. That's not going to make or break your relationship with that particular restaurant; however, when the bill finally comes and you are ready to either pay with Apple Pay or your credit card and the server tells you, "Sorry, we only accept cash," this event will break your relationship with that particular restaurant. Most people don't carry cash nowadays, so this scenario would make the end of a great night not so pleasant.

Moments of truth are so important to identify. If you don't identify them, you will lose your customers in a heartbeat. You don't have all the resources to fix every problem at once, so knowing the moments of truth will help you prioritize which problems you want to fix first.

7. **Jobs-to-be-Done:** What is Sally trying to do? It's important to keep that in mind. Your solution will help your customer do this job faster and better; however, it will be through a completely different method than what she is accustomed to. This is when your customer's challenges become irrelevant because you are innovating the job that Sally used to do in the only way she knew how. *(Refer to Chapter 2: What Do They Want to Do?)*

8. **Challenges:** What are the challenges that Sally faces trying to do the jobs she wants to do? Identify your customer's problems by simply asking them what their challenges are. Whether you chose the qualitative or quantitative method, it doesn't matter. It's important to keep these challenges visible at all times.

9. **Delights:** Just like you laid out all of what upsets your customer, you want to understand what makes her delighted. What makes Sally happy and satisfied?

10. **Emotions:** What is she feeling right at that step? Is she wowed, frustrated, happy, angry, anxious, or excited? Would her emotions drive her to take follow-up action or put her at a standstill? Or worse, drive her away?

11. **Channels:** How is she interacting with you? Is it by phone? Your website? Your store?

12. **Tools:** What tools is she using throughout her journey to achieve what she wants to achieve? Does she use any products or services, including yours? Does she use your competition's products and services? For example, if she is paying, is she

using Apple Pay? Credit card or cash? Does she search for more information on your product using her phone?

13. **Improvement Opportunities:** You might have already started thinking about how you can improve the customer's experience based on the challenges you have identified, your customer's delights, and their jobs-to-be-done. This is where you jot down everything down to refer to it in your ideation sessions and when planning how to help your customers with their problems.

You want to think about every step of the way, from the moment Sally starts thinking of what she wants to do to when she finds you, buys your product, and uses it.

There are many tools out there to help you create a fancy-looking Journey Map, but honestly, you have all you need. You can use a good classic spreadsheet for it. All you have to do is create different rows for each component and start creating the journey stages and steps for your chosen persona. Once you complete the end-to-end journey, you can begin filling out the rest of the components, and you will be left with a complete Journey Map.

If you want to take it further, you can certainly use Journey Mapping tools such as smaply (smaply.com) to beautify it and add spice. You can also add cartoons to create a visualization aspect to it and bring the journey to life. You can even hang it on your wall. That being said, it's not necessary to do all that. Sometimes you need to because you want to involve other people in the thinking process. Other times, it's okay to have it in a rough format. It's all up to you.

By mapping your customer's journey, you will be able to visualize and understand when your customer feels pain in doing the job she needs to get done. You will understand her challenges and emotional journey, even if your product did not cause her despair. It will help you uncover opportunities in which you can serve her better.

Suppose you can't serve her in the opportunities you have uncovered because perhaps they are not related to your core product. In this case, you can partner with someone else or at the very least recommend some solutions to your customers. They will love it and appreciate you for it.

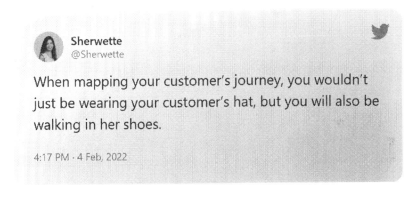

Sherwette
@Sherwette

When mapping your customer's journey, you wouldn't just be wearing your customer's hat, but you will also be walking in her shoes.

4:17 PM · 4 Feb, 2022

Note: The above-mentioned items are not set in stone. You can add or remove any of the layers depending on the nature of the project and its purpose.

Mystery Shopping: *How do you validate your understanding of the customer journey?*

After you are finished mapping your customer's journey, you can conduct one of my also very favorite customer research methods: **Mystery Shopping.** It allows you to you literally walk in your customer's shoes

> **Mystery Shopping** is when you pretend to be the customer. You do exactly what she would do to understand how well she is being served and identify areas that need improvement.

Let's take the example of buying coffee beans. When conducting mystery shopping, I want to buy the coffee beans from the store.

What will I do?

1. I drive my car and follow Google Maps.
2. I find the store, but I can't find parking.
3. I keep on driving around the store for 15 minutes trying to find parking.

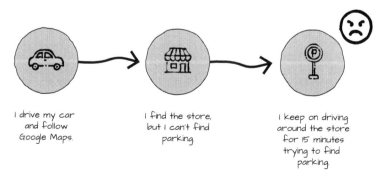

I drive my car and follow Google Maps.

I find the store, but I can't find parking.

I keep on driving around the store for 15 minutes trying to find parking.

From a customer experience perspective, it's not the best. Finding parking has nothing to do with the quality of beans or the activity of making coffee at home. But, it is frustrating. I might end up just buying something completely different to avoid struggling to find a parking space.

In this case, an opportunity arises. For example, as the retailer could provide delivery options so that I wouldn't have to go to the store. Another alternative would be for the retailer to partner with supermarkets so their coffee bean products are more accessible to their customers. They could even provide a drive-through option, completely eliminating the problem of parking.

Don't forget, though, the mystery shopping exercise helped you go through the customer experience, so if and when you uncover new insights, add them to the challenges, delights, and tools sections in your Journey Map. You may revisit other components. Your customer journey is a live document, and it's not to be forgotten in a lonely folder on your computer. -Sherwette

Chapter Quiz

Congratulations on making it through Chapter 4! By now, you should genuinely know what keeps your customers up at night and what challenges are stopping them from getting what they want.

Think you're ready for a chapter quiz?

True/False

1: People don't change the way they do things. (True/False)

2: When analyzing your customer research, it's best to segment customers based on their demographics to accurately represent their views. (True/False)

Quiz Answer Key

Answer 1: False. Behavioral change is a thing. To bring about behavioral change, motivation and ease have to both be present.

Answer 2: False. Customer segmentation by demographics alone will not provide you with insights you can use to better build your products. Instead, it's best to segment customers based on their jobs-to-be-done, challenges, and demographical data.

Putting It All into Action

Insight without action is useless. It's time to investigate what is stopping your customers from buying your product, for real, and put that knowledge to use.

Here's your checklist:

1. Ask your customers about their challenges.
2. Map your customer Journey Map.
3. Conduct a mystery shopping exercise to uncover more insights about your customer's experience.

You're almost halfway through this book and well on your way to learning why no one is buying your product, so keep going! And, if you haven't designed your product yet, then it's great you wanted to do things the right way. In Chapter 5, we're going to explore your value proposition and nail down what problem you're helping your customers solve.

References

1. Tori Sorenson. "The Great BRAIN Cleanse Quotes Images to Share and Download." Quoteslyfe. Accessed 2021. https://www.quoteslyfe.com/author/Toni-Sorenson-The-Great-Brain-Cleanse-quotes.
2. Adam Ferrier, and Fleming, Jennifer. The Advertising Effect: How to Change Behaviour. South Melbourne, Vic.: Oxford University Press, 2014.
3. Ferrier, "The Advertising Effect," 2014.
4. Ferrier, "The Advertising Effect," 2014.
5. Ryan Levesque. Ask. Hay House Inc, 2019, https://askmethod.com/.

CHAPTER 5

What Problem Are You Helping Them Solve?

"Customers don't buy products;
they pull them into their life to make progress."
—Clayton Christensen[1]

Chapter Objectives:

- **Value Proposition**: What is it?
- **Finding the Fit**: How do you find your value proposition?
- **Case Study**: Hello Chef

After COVID-19 hit and quarantine became our reality, there were some major adjustments to be made. Like many others, I became extra paranoid about touching anything outside the house, let alone eat anything not made in my kitchen. Needless to say, restaurants suffered drastically during lockdown.

Before COVID, my schedule was pretty busy, and I was usually never home. As a result, I rarely ate at home. When I was home, I would order take-out, using apps like Zomato, Deliveroo, and Uber Eats.

But when the pandemic hit and the only "safe" way for me to eat was to cook my own food, I had to go to the grocery store, buy some ingredients, and experiment with my very own recipes.

At first, it was fun. And, where could I go anyway? We weren't allowed to go anywhere, other than the supermarket, pharmacy, and hospital when needed.

So, I tried some of my own inventions. I called my mom to ask about her recipes which, for the most part, I couldn't do as good as her for some reason. I just couldn't top my mom's food.

Eventually, I got tired of the whole process of deciding what to eat, buying it, and cooking every day. I wanted to be efficient, so I bought the ingredients in bulk, prepared the same exact dishes in huge portions, divided them into smaller portions for daily meals, and put them in the freezer. That way, whenever I wanted to cook something, I could just get it out of my freezer, put it in the oven, and it was ready to go.

It worked for a while, until I got sick of my own food.

Don't get me wrong. I love cooking, but I kind of get tired of eating the same thing over and over again. Not to mention that I hate deciding on a dish, grocery shopping, and doing the dishes afterward. I really hate doing the dishes.

And so, one day, I was browsing LinkedIn and found a company called "Hello Chef" advertising for a job, and I stopped there for a moment and asked, *"What is Hello Chef?"* One would think I had found out about Hello Chef from a typical advertisement, but the universe works in mysterious ways.

I checked out their website and found out that all I had to do was choose my own recipes, and they would buy the ingredients in the right portions and send them right to my doorstep. I got excited and wanted to try it. I wasn't sure if it was something I really wanted to do, but I did it. They had a very generous discount for first-time subscribers.

And my God, when I tried it, it was the best food I had ever cooked in my entire life. It was high-end restaurant quality dishes cooked in my very own kitchen with my very own hands. The food was delicious. The meat was fresh. I mean, not once when I bought fresh meat in Dubai did it taste good—not until I got it from Hello Chef. Not only do they send the ingredients in the exact portions, but the recipes are so detailed, and the steps are by the minute. I didn't have to think for a second about what I needed to do next.

Sure, it's more expensive than going to the grocery store and buying the ingredients myself. But who has the time? Plus, I don't usually have all the ingredients that are unique to the Thai and Indian dishes I love in my kitchen. I also don't want to have bottles of Indian herbs lined up in my kitchen if I don't cook that cuisine that often. Chances are that I would cook those dishes only a few times.

I guess Hello Chef found the sweet spot with their ideal customers and relieved many of their pains, such as finding out what to cook, buying groceries, and smashing the boredom out of eating the same dish over and over again.

Having said that, I am guessing that their ideal customer is not me. This is because they don't offer any options for people who live alone. The minimum you can order is for two people, and you have to order four dishes per week, so for me, that means eight meals per week. That's a lot of food for one person. So I guess it was catered more towards couples or families. I live alone, and because the food was so good, I wanted to share it with the people I love, so I started inviting friends over for dinner. Unfortunately, it's not very sustainable for me to plan my life around inviting people over to have a fantastic dinner. Hello Chef's plan didn't work for me in the long-term, so I only occasionally ordered a week's menu when I wanted to indulge in restaurant-quality home cooking.

I am not the ideal customer, but I happen to really love their product. I recommend it to many of my friends. Maybe, just maybe, they could create a value proposition canvas catered to customers like myself.

Wait, what is a value proposition canvas?

The **value proposition canvas**[2] is a tool developed by Dr. Alexander Osterwalder, co-founder of Strategyzer, that helps you ensure your product or service is centered on customer values and needs.

You can use this tool when you ideate a new product, start from scratch, refine an existing product, or completely revamp your product. The value proposition canvas helps you understand your product, how it fits your customers, the jobs they want to do, and their desires.

Value Proposition: *What is it?*

Value proposition is how your products or services help your customer. To sell, <u>your customer profile and your Value Map must be compatible.</u>

Value proposition simply answers this question: **Why would customers buy from you? Why would they want to do business with you?**

And it looks like this:

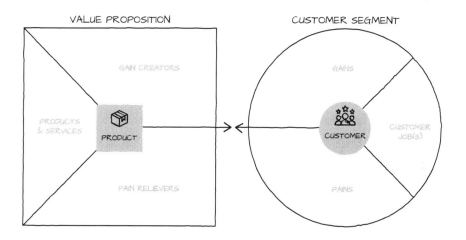

The Value Proposition Canvas
Source: Strategyzer by Dr. Alexander Osterwalder

You can have a value proposition canvas for each customer segment *(Refer to Chapter 1: Who Do You Want to Serve?)*. In fact, you can have more than one canvas for each segment based on the personas you have created. The goal is to have one focused value proposition per canvas.

Tip:

> You can have more than one persona for each customer segment. For example, suppose your customer segment is busy, single individuals who want to eat healthy. In this case, you can have a persona who wants to eat more protein and have more calorie intake to build muscles, and you can have another persona who wants to cut down on calories and lose weight. You can also have a third persona who decided to go vegan and just wants to maintain their weight.

Each value proposition canvas has two components:

1. **Customer Profile** - On the right side of the canvas, you will find a circle that includes your customer's profile (a specific segment of your customers) where you can jot down the following:

   • **Jobs-to-be-Done** - What is she trying to get done? In her work and her life? (*Refer to Chapter 2: What Do They Want to Do?*)

   • **Gains** - What does success look like? What are the outcomes she wants or the benefits she is seeking? (*Refer to Chapter 2: What Do They Want to Do? & Chapter 3: Why Do They Want to Do It?*)

   • **Pains** - What does failure look like? What are the adverse outcomes, risks, and obstacles related to the Jobs-to-be-Done? (*Refer to Chapter 4: What Is Stopping Them?*)

2. **Value Map** - On the left side of the canvas, place your product and brainstorm how it will help your customers. This includes the features of a specific value proposition in your business. You will find a square that includes your:

- **Products and Services** - What products and services is your value proposition built around? Your products could be:
  - *Physical or Tangible Products:* Actual goods that you buy.
  - *Digital Products:* Anything from music downloads to e-books to online memberships, courses, or access to software tools.
  - *Intangible Products:* Services or experiences, like as after-sales support, cleaning services, or haircuts.
  - *Financial Products and Services:* Anything from financing, payment plans, retirement planning, or even Bitcoin investments.
- **Gain Creators** – How do your products and services create customer gains? How do they make her happier?
- **Pain Relievers** – How do your products and services alleviate customer pains?

It's about how your products or services help your customers. And to sell, you <u>must have a fit between your customer profile and Value Map</u>.

List your customer's jobs-to-be-done, their pains, and their gains. List your products and services, your gain creators, and pain relievers. Just know that you are not obligated or expected to help your customer with all her jobs, nor all her issues. She may have her expectations, but she knows that she can't have it all. And as much as you want to help her, she also knows that you couldn't possibly alleviate all her pains.

So, what to do?

Focus on her biggest pains, the headaches that keep her up at night. You want to look at your Value Map, your products and services, your pain relievers and gain creators, and ask yourself:

- *Am I helping my customer do her job faster and better?*
- *Am I addressing her essential gains?*
- *Am I addressing her extreme pains?*

When answering the above questions, you are figuring out your fit. You want to find the fit.

The fit?

The fit is the core of your value proposition. It's what gets your customer excited about your product. Why? Because you have crafted your art. You are helping your customer do her job better and faster. You have addressed what's most important to her, the jobs she wants to get done. You alleviated her extreme pains and created gains that she cares about.

There are three kinds of fit, or shall we call them, stages of your fit:

1. **Problem-Solution Fit: On Paper** - This is when you *think* you have found the value proposition. You understand the customer's jobs, pains, and gains and assumed that your

products and services will act as gain creators and pain relievers to your customer. But will they?

2. **Product Market Fit: With Your Customers** - This is when you get proof that your customers *care* and are truly passionate about what you are offering. How do you know? They are buying. *(More on that in Chapter 8: Are You Really Helping Them?)* You are gaining traction in the market but not necessarily making a profit. You have buying customers, which proves that what you are offering provides them with real value. Or, perhaps, they don't care about your value proposition, so you have to go back to the drawing board and think again.

3. **Business Model Fit: Making Money** - This is when you have gone beyond simply becoming known in the market to actually making a profit. Your revenue exceeds your costs and you have built a sustainable business model that is profitable and scalable.

Your value proposition starts out being a hypothesis. Only after being tested with paying clients does it become viable. Then, once you start making money, it's where you know you have hit the sweet spot.

Once you figure out your value proposition, you will be able to write value proposition statement in that format:

We help (X Customers) do (Y jobs) by doing (Z product/service).

Tips:

- When working with your Value Map, make sure to think about your products and services, gain creators and pain relievers from a relevant point of view to your customer. Some of them are absolutely essential for your customer, while others will be considered just "nice to have." Keeping that in mind will help you prioritize where you need to focus your efforts.

- If you are a team or even working solo, one of the best ways to ignite your ideas is to move and write with pen and paper. You can print those value proposition canvases and use sticky notes to jot down all your ideas.

Finding the Fit: *How do you find your value proposition?*

Filling in the right side of the canvas should be straightforward since you have already done the work. Just be sure not to overwhelm yourself. Don't try to put EVERYTHING on one canvas. Remember, you need to create one canvas per customer segment. You can have more than one canvas per segment depending on the market you are serving (multiple personas), the product you are offering, or the value proposition you are delivering as part of that product.

Tip:

Access templates for the value proposition canvas by Strategyzer here: https://platform.strategyzer.com/resources.

Now comes the fun part, the **brainstorming session.**

Okay, great. Where to start?

First, choose your customer segment and persona for a specific value proposition canvas.

1. **Build your Customer Profile:** Your customer persona
   - Choose the jobs-to-be-done for this persona
   - Add the gains (their expected outcomes and desires)
   - Add the pains (their challenges)
2. **Build your Value Map:** Your product
   - Describe your product or service
   - List gain creators - *How will your product help them achieve their expected outcomes and desires?*
   - List the pain relievers - *How will your product or service help your customers overcome their challenges?*
   - Rank your products and services, gain creators and pain relievers in order of importance according to your customer
3. **Find the Fit:** Your value proposition
   - Map your gain creators and pain relievers from the Value Map to the customer profile's jobs, gains, or pains
     - Go through your **pain relievers** one by one and check if they fit a customer job, pain, or gain
     - Go through your **gain creators** one by one and check if they fit a customer job, pain, or gain
4. **Test your Fit:** (*Refer to Chapter 8: Are You Really Helping Them?*)

Tips:

- Use sticky notes. You want to play around, remove, add, or scratch an idea altogether with all the flexibility you can have. And don't forget to make the best out of the sticky notes' colors! You can use, for example, yellow sticky notes for the jobs-to-be-done and your products or service, pink ones for the pains, and green ones for the gains. That way, you can spot right away what idea relates to what.

- Use digital collaboration tools. The pandemic introduced new ways of working. In today's world, most of us work remotely. Others work some combination of remote and in-office. Tools such as MIRO (https://www.miro.com) or MURAL (https://www.mural.co) can help you simulate the sticky note workshop setting online and get input from everyone participating in this exercise.

- Invite your customers or your team that interacts with customers. Customer insights will not come by status or years of experience but from those who interact with your customers firsthand. So make sure to invite a few participants who speak with your customers day-in and day-out. Even better, if you can, invite a few customers to get their insights firsthand.

Case Study: *Hello Chef*

As I mentioned earlier at the beginning of this chapter, although I am absolutely in love with Hello Chef's products, I might not be the ideal customer just yet, just like Sally from Chapter 1. For one simple reason, it wasn't meant for individuals who live alone. We will look deeper into the needs of Sally, who lives alone, in comparison with Mark, who has a family—making him the perfect customer for Hello Chef. That said, both Sally and I could be the perfect customers for Hello Chef if their product were tweaked a little to fit the needs of customers who live alone.

Who is the ideal customer?

It's families and couples who want to cook dinner four days a week and enjoy a home-cooked meal.

So, with that in mind, let's answer some of the questions we have discussed in the book so far and figure out why I am not an ideal customer and how I could be.

1. Who is the customer?
2. What do they want to do?
3. Why do they want to do it?
4. What is stopping them?

Customer Segment #1: Sally – Not the current ideal customer.

Who is the customer?

Sally: Works as a creative director in an advertising agency, a demanding job that leaves her with little time for herself. She lives in Dubai and doesn't have much time to think about eating, buying, and cooking. She lives alone. She also pursues her other passions besides work and enjoys spending quality time with her friends.

What does she want to do?
- Cook and eat healthy, delicious, low-calorie food at home during the week.
- Go out to eat during the week for business dinners and friends' get-togethers.
- Stay fit.
- Invite some friends and her fiancé over for dinner for a delicious home-cooked meal, perhaps also during the weekend.

Why does she want to do it?
- She loves to enjoy food and savor it.
- She wants to know what she is eating because she wants to stay healthy and fit.
- She loves to invite her friends and her fiancé over for dinner because she enjoys having them around.

What is stopping her?
- She doesn't have enough time to go grocery shopping.
- She uses grocery shopping apps, but she can't always find

what she needs and spends a lot of time, sometimes up to an hour, trying to figure out which shop to get all the ingredients for recipes she found on the internet.

- She wants to lose weight and stay fit and doesn't know if ordering ready-made "healthy" meals is actually healthy.
- She spends hours agonizing over what to cook.
- The internet has so many recipes she doesn't know which ones to choose.
- The recipes she likes on the internet have ingredients she doesn't know where to find.
- She would use some of the ingredients once and doesn't want to get a whole bottle or box for one recipe.
- She hates doing the dishes.
- Whenever she buys meat in Dubai, it tastes like plastic.
- She doesn't know how to pick the right cut of meat or fish.
- She doesn't want to cook the same dishes over and over.
- She doesn't know how to portion out ingredients if she wants to scale the meal and cook for more people (let's say four people instead of one or two people).

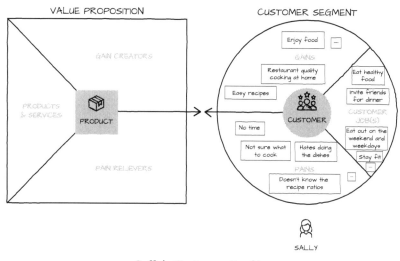

Sally's Customer Profile

Customer Segment #2: Mark - The current ideal customer.

Who is the customer?

Mark: An executive, married, with two kids. His wife also works a full-time job, leaving them very little time to think about what to eat, buy, or cook. He traveled quite a bit with his wife before settling in Dubai, and they love to enjoy food from all over the world. He spends the weekend with his family going out and doing family activities, and during the week, they are pretty busy working and helping the kids out with their homework. He likes to alternate cooking days with his wife, and although they both are good cooks, the number of recipes they know how to perfect is quite limited. However, he loves cooking for his family and even has the kids help out. He is very particular about what he and his family eat and has adopted a vegan lifestyle.

What does he want to do?
- Cook together with his family.
- Ensure his family is eating healthy, delicious food.
- Eat out on the weekend.

Why does he want to do it?
- Enjoy dinner with family.
- Eat healthy food.
- Ensure his family is eating healthy food.
- Bond with his family.

What is stopping him?

- He has little time to plan, buy, and prepare food.
- Vegan food recipes he is familiar with are very limited.
- He is bored with cooking the same meals over and over.
- The kids are bored with eating the same foods over and over.

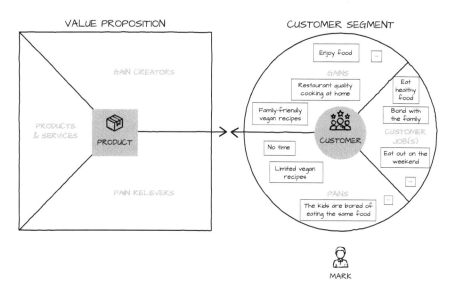

Mark's Customer Profile

Now, let's think about how Hello Chef is helping both of those customer segments with their product.

- Customer Segment #1: Sally - Not the current ideal customer.
- Customer Segment #2: Mark - The current ideal customer.

Hello Chef Product Value for Sally and Mark

		Sally	Mark
Product/ Service	Offers classic and choice boxes	✓	✓
	Classic Box allows you to choose from nine recipes		
	Choice Box allows you to choose from 20 recipes	✓	✓
	Each week there are fresh, new recipes prepared by the chef, offering different categories, such as family-friendly, calorie-smart, vegan, dairy-free, gluten-free, and gourmet (which is the premium dish for a slightly higher price per serving)	✓	✓
	Allows you to choose among 2, 3, and 4 people to serve		✓
	Delivers four meals a week based on the preferred days		✓
	Provides flexible commitment and the ability to skip weeks in case you are out of town	✓	✓
Gain creators	The recipes are so detailed by the minute that you wouldn't have to think for a second what to do next	✓	✓
	Includes fresh, new recipes every week	✓	✓
	Includes recipes from around the world	✓	✓
	Includes a premium dish every week to have a gourmet food experience at home	✓	✓
	Includes recipes that can be cooked in as little as 20 minutes or up to 50 minutes, depending on how much time you want to dedicate to cooking	✓	✓
Pain relievers	Choose recipes from the comfort of your couch every week	✓	✓
	The ingredients and recipes will be delivered to your doorstep on specific days of the week at the time of your choosing, such as dawn, morning, afternoon, or evening, based on your preference	✓	✓

		Sally	Mark
Pain relievers	You don't have to do the shopping or spend hours on grocery apps trying to figure out if you have the right ingredients.	✓	✓
	Includes different options for recipes such as family-friendly, calorie-smart, dairy-free, gluten-free, and vegan for special dietary requirements	✓	✓
	Includes fast and easy recipes that can be created in as little as 20 minutes	✓	✓
Possible gain creators for Sally	Ability to deliver some meals only for one person and other meals for two or more people	✓	
	Ability to deliver meals 2-3 days a week instead of 4 in case she is planning outings	✓	
	Ability to choose only two dishes for two people per week instead of 4	✓	
Possible pain relievers for Mark	More family-friendly vegan dishes		✓

You see, the gain creators and pain relievers actually apply to both customer segments, and with a few twists, a whole new customer segment, such as Sally, could be added to the consistent subscribers of this service.

Please view the below value proposition canvases for illustrative purposes. You can start populating your value proposition canvas based on your products and services, and remember, use sticky notes or online collaboration tools such as Miro (Miro.com) or Mural (Mural.com).

Sally's Persona Value Proposition Canvas:

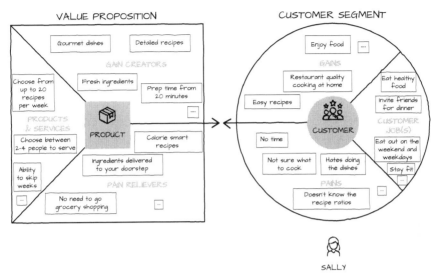

Sally's Value Proposition Canvas

Mark's Persona Value Proposition Canvas:

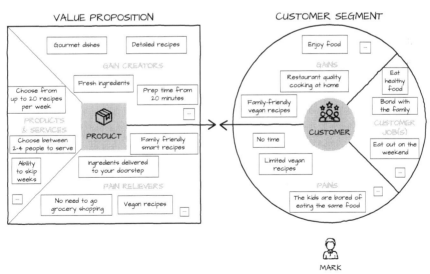

Mark's Value Proposition Canvas

Chapter Quiz

Congratulations on making it through Chapter 5! Did you start thinking about what problem you are helping your customers solve?

You know the drill. Ready to test your knowledge with a chapter quiz?

True/False

1: You can only have one value proposition canvas for your business. (True/False)

2: A value proposition fit can have a logical problem-solution fit on paper but still not pass the product-market fit with your customers. (True/False)

Quiz Answer Key

Answer 1: False. You can have as many value proposition canvases as you need. You can create more than one for each customer segment based on the different services and products you offer.

Answer 2: True. A problem-solution fit is an initial hypothesis that you have brainstormed with your team and customers about possible solutions to their problems. However, product-market fit is proof that your product solves customer problems—when they start spending money and buying your product, and when you start making a profit. A business model fit is when your revenue exceeds your costs, and you can build a sustainable business model that is profitable and scalable.

Putting It All into Action

In the previous chapters, you were all in, trying to get to know your customers better. And now, in this chapter, you should see how all the previous research works for your specific product. It's time to put it all into action and be clear on your value proposition.

Here's your checklist:

1. Choose your customer persona and build the customer profile canvas based on the jobs-to-be-done, gains, and pains.
2. Build your Value Map for your product or service and list the gain creators and pain relievers you offer.
3. Rank the order of importance of your products/services, gain creators, and pain relievers according to your customers.
4. Find the fit by mapping the gain creators and pain relievers from the Value Map to your customer's profile jobs, gains, and pains.
5. Test your fit against the characteristics of great value propositions.
6. Test your problem-solution fit.
7. Test your market fit. *(More on that in Chapter 8: Are You Really Helping Them?)*
8. Test your business model fit. *(More on that in Chapter 8: Are You Really Helping Them?)*

Now that you have finished Chapter 5 and have an idea of how your product will serve your customers, you're ready to find out where you stand with your customers among the competition. Next, in Chapter 6, we're going to explore where you and your products and services look compared to your competition in the market. Will your products rank better or worse? Will you charge more or less? Well, let's go find out!

References

1. Clayton Christensen. "Clay Christensen's Jobs-to-be-Done Theory Framework." FullStory, April 9, 2020. https://www.fullstory.com/blog/clayton-christensen-jobs-to-be-done-framework-product-development.
2. Alexander Osterwalder. "Value Proposition Canvas – Download the Official Template." Strategyzer, n.d. https://www.strategyzer.com/canvas/value-proposition-canvas.

CHAPTER 6

How Does Your Product Compare
to Other Products on the Market?

"To find a unique position, you must ignore conventional logic. Conventional logic says you find your concept inside yourself or inside the product. Not true. What you must do is look inside the prospect's mind."

-Al Ries[1]

Chapter Objectives:

- **Your Position in the Market**: Is your product better or worse? Do you charge more or less?
- **Performance and Quality**: Will your product help your customer do her job better or worse?
- **Price Compared to the Competition**: Is your product more or less expensive than the market?
- **Product Strategy**: What is your product strategy based on quality and price?

Do you use Google Maps when you drive?

I know I do. I almost always put Google Maps navigation on my phone while driving, whether I know how to get where I am going or not.

In fact, I am almost 100% certain that I am under the behavioral bias of the Google effect or digital amnesia.

What is the Google effect?

It's when we let go of remembering routes. Because we know we can have information at our fingertips, our memory selects not to remember specific details. Basically, when we expect we will need certain information in the future, instead of recalling the information, we recall how we can access it. So, in this case, Google Maps.

That worked well for years with me, at least until Google Maps decided to start having performance issues right when I had no idea which exit I was supposed to take on the highway.

I don't like it when the application lags. I don't know if it's because the Google Maps app is acting a little crazy or because my phone is a bit old (or at least not the latest model). The reason actually doesn't matter. What matters is that I know I can't rely on Google Maps like I used to.

So, what did I do instead? Perhaps I could make it a point to become more consciously familiar with the routes I need to take. But if you knew anything about me, you would know that my sense of direction is a lost cause.

Long story short, I did not memorize routes, but I did start using Apple Maps.

Wait. What?

Yes, I am a loyal Google Maps customer, but whenever my Google Maps freezes up, I calmly close it and open my Apple Maps, which works perfectly fine. My Apple Watch even vibrates 300 meters before I need to take an exit so I am alert, never having to miss an exit again.

You see, I would have never thought to use Apple Maps until Google Maps disappointed me. And we all know these are the two main tycoons of the tech industry. Even so, Google is not perfect.

One of the reasons customers switch from one product to another is quality, and this should not be taken lightly.

It's not like all of Apple's attempts to convert me as a customer for some of their other products were entirely successful. For example, most people I know use Spotify, iTunes, or Soundcloud to listen to music.

I use an app called Anghami instead. I love it simply because it has English and Arabic music, even though iTunes has Arabic music. It just never compares when it comes to the diversity of the collection. Actually, Apple gave me a free 6-month trial for iTunes so I could try it and possibly switch to them, but I didn't. I still use Anghami; it's the best music app for me. So far, Anghami hasn't upset me, and the quality is pretty decent.

Quality is not the only reason customers switch from using one product to another. Price plays a large role as well.

Under some circumstances, customers will give up quality for price. Remember that incredible apartment with the breathtaking view of the canal that I moved to post-COVID because I wanted the space to be creative so I could paint, write, and exercise?

I moved out of it while writing this book, actually. I stayed one year, and as it turned out, I didn't use all the facilities there. I didn't use the pool or the gym as much as I wanted to. I worked most of the time. And for a good few months, I went back home to be with my mother, so I wasn't even at the apartment.

Even though it's a fantastic apartment, I decided to move. Why? Well, because:
1. It was expensive, and ...
2. I knew I wouldn't be in Dubai long enough to enjoy it.

As vaccines became available and things began going back to normal(-ish), I started traveling most of the week to see clients again. So, I decided to move to another, also lovely, apartment in the same area I lived in, just not as nice as the one with the view, but it was all I needed—and it was less expensive.

Understanding your market and product alone wouldn't be enough. You want to know what your competition is doing and where you stand in the market, so you are clear in your head if you will provide your customers with better/worse quality products or more expensive/cheaper products.

Your Position in the Market: *Is your product better or worse? Do you charge more or less?*

You need to figure out your position compared to your competition with respect to two main factors:

1. **Performance and Quality:** Your product's performance and quality compared to the competition. Does your product or service help your customer do a job better or worse than your competition?

2. **Price:** Your price compared to your competition. Is your price more or less expensive than the competition?

Why do you need to know this?

Because customers buy when you help them get the job done:

1. **Better** (faster, more predictably, with higher output) and/or
2. **More cheaply**

So, what does this mean?

There are four possibilities that you could offer your customers, and Tony Ulwick, in his book *Jobs-to-be-Done*, outlined this in a framework called **Jobs-to-Be-Done Growth Strategy Matrix.**[2]

You can create products or services that fall in one of the following categories:

1. Better and more expensive
2. Better and less expensive
3. Worse and less expensive

4. Worse and more expensive

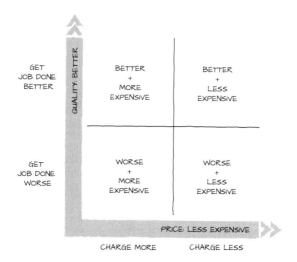

Source: Jobs-to-be-Done by Tony Ulwick

Let's talk about that for a bit.

Performance and Quality: *Will your product help your customer do her job better or worse?*

Everyone loves quick results.

In fact, in my consulting world, almost all my clients are always looking out for those "quick win" initiatives whenever they have a 3- or 5-year-roadmap strategy.

A quick win gives instant gratification.

An instant feel-good reward.

Your customer wants to hear "well done" whispered in her ear every moment possible.

The dreams your customer wants to achieve. The things she wants to do. They drive her every waking moment. They fuel her day.

She can't do it all by herself, so she looks for help.

It could be you. It could be your competition.

What you want to understand is ... **How well is she served?**

How well is she doing the job that she wants to do?

Remember the challenges we were uncovering in Chapter 4? *(What Is Stopping Them?)*

Those challenges will tell you if your customer is *under*-**served** or *over*-**served**.

Again, there are four types of customers who are underserved or overserved. Let's have a look.

1] Non-customers

Who are they?

- Customers who are not attempting to get the job done because they can't afford any of the products in the market.
- Customers who are using solutions not in the market.

What can you do about it?

- Offer: *A worse-performing, less expensive product.*

2] Customers with limited or no alternatives

Who are they?

- Customers who don't have a choice in a product because of the limitations imposed upon them. Think about the airport bar and how overpriced it is.

What can you do about it?

- Offer: *A worse-performing, more expensive product.*

3] Overserved customers

Who are they?
- Customers with no unmet needs.

What can you do about it?
- Offer: *A better-performing, less expensive product.*

4] Underserved customers

Who are they?
- Customers with **unmet need**s and willing to pay more to get the job done better.

What can you do about it?
- Offer:
  - Better performing product.
  - Better performing, more expensive product.

One thing to keep in mind, though, is your strategy on whether you decide to go after overserved or underserved customers. It may apply to your products or services; it doesn't apply to your whole company. So, you can start offering one product to one type of customer, then move on to another type of customer with a different kind of product, catering to their needs and jobs-to-be-done.
- If they are **overserved, you have to help them get the job done better, more efficiently, and with fewer issues.**
- If they are **underserved, you can help them get the job done.** Period. Going a step further and helping them get the job done better and faster will win the hearts of everyone.

Go easy on yourself, though. You don't have to be the *best* when you're starting out. If you don't have the resources that will allow you to get the job done in the best way, you can start with the underserved customers.

Summary of Customer Types

Customer type	Who are they?	What can you do about it?
1] Non-customers	Customers who are not attempting to get the job done because they can't afford any of the products in the market. Customers who are using solutions not in the market.	Offer: *A worse-performing, less expensive product.*
2] Customers with limited or no alternatives	Customers who don't have a choice in a product because of the limitations imposed upon them (like when you have to buy an expensive drink at the airport bar or an overpriced water bottle on the plane).	Offer: *A worse-performing, more expensive product.*
3] Overserved customers	Customers with no unmet needs.	Offer: *A better-performing, less expensive product.*
4] Underserved customers	Customers with unmet needs willing to pay more to get the job done better.	Offer: • *Better performing product.* • *Better performing, more expensive product.*

Be sure to also jot down what your competition is doing in each of those quadrants respectively.

- **Competition helping <u>overserved</u> customers**
  - Competitor: Who is helping the overserved customers?
  - Product: How are they helping them get the job done better?
  - Quality: How well are they serving them?

- **Competition helping <u>underserved</u> customers**
  - Competitor: Who is helping the underserved customers?
  - Product: How are they helping them get the job done?
  - Quality: How well are they serving them?

Understand your customers, yourself, and your competition.

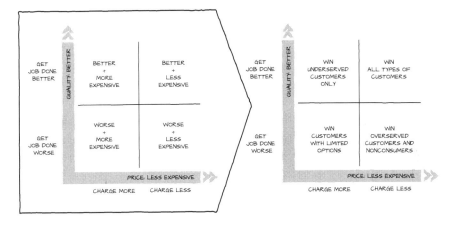

Source: Jobs-to-be-Done by Tony Ulwick

Price Compared to the Competition: *Is your product more or less expensive than the market?*

Let's face it; when you are starting out, you might not be the best ... and that's OKAY.

In fact, most "A" players start out that way. They start with what little they do know.

If you know very little, just charge less.

But remember, always bring value.

If you are experienced in your craft, even better.

You see, not all customers you serve are on the same sophistication level. For example, if you're helping someone just starting to discover cooking and you provide him with ingredients and nutrition information, your guidance will be incredibly valuable. If, however, you are serving someone with a very high sophistication level who has been cooking for years and has cooked a variety of recipes from vegan to vegetarian to keto, you teaching him the basics of the nutrition and how to prepare the ingredients wouldn't give him much value.

(Refer to Chapter 9: Do They Know about It? to learn more about your customer awareness and sophistication stages.)

The below chart can give you an idea of where you stand next to your competition. Jot down your competition and see where you fit.

Answer these questions:

- **Competition helping <u>overserved</u> customers**
    - Competitor: Who is helping the overserved customers?
    - Product: How are they helping them get the job done better?
    - Quality: How well are they serving them?
    - Price: How much are they charging?

- **Competition helping <u>underserved</u> customers**
    - Competitor: Who is helping the underserved customers?
    - Product: How are they helping them get the job done?
    - Quality: How well are they serving them?
    - Price: How much are they charging?

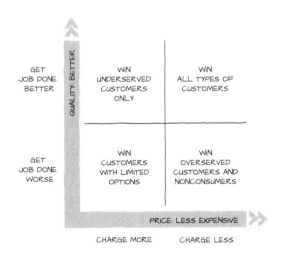

Source: Jobs-to-be-Done by Tony Ulwick

Based on what we just discussed, by now, you should know:

1. If your customers are overserved or underserved.
2. If your product or service will help your customer do the job better.
3. If your product or service will be more or less expensive than the market.
4. Where you stand compared to the competition.

Product Strategy: *What is your product strategy based on quality and price?*

Now that you understand where you stand compared to your competition regarding quality and price, let's talk about your **product strategy.**

Tony Ulwick outlined five different strategies that you can apply toward your products.[3]

1] Differentiated Strategy

- **Customer:** Underserved consumers *(customers with unmet needs who are willing to pay more to get the job done better).*
- **Quality:** Job done MUCH better.
- **Price:** Much more expensive (up to 10x).
- **When to use it**
  - 1. When you can provide **superior performance and quality** compared to your competition by targeting a small percentage of the market share at a **premium price.**
  - 2. When you want to enter the market at a high end and slowly move down the market by offering cheaper options of their products, by either making older products cheaper when introducing new versions or by creating specific cheaper versions for other segments of the market.

- **Examples:**
  - Nespresso's coffee machine
  - Apple's iPhone
  - Peloton
  - Organic food products
  - Dyson's vacuum cleaner

2] Dominant Strategy

- **Customer:** All types of customers (overserved & underserved)
- **Quality:** Job done much (20%) better
- **Price:** Cheaper (20%)
- **When to use it:** When you are **new to the market**. You create a product that **does the job better** than the competition ... And it's **cheaper**. You are already miles away from your competition. They will have to cut their margins and invest their time, money, and resources to reach your quality. And when they do, you would have already penetrated the market.
- **Examples:**
  - Google search
  - Netflix streaming videos

3] Disruptive Strategy

- **Customer:** Overserved customers (customers with no unmet needs) or non-consumers with a new product or service.
- **Quality:** Not as good as the competition.

- **Price:** Much cheaper than what's offered in the market.
- **When to use it:** When you can provide **the basic job to be done much cheaper** than the competition. You tap into the overserved customers who don't mind having less features in the product to save money and the non-customers who couldn't afford to buy the other products in the market.
- **Examples:**
  - Google Docs as compared Microsoft Office
  - Coursera compared to traditional education
  - Canva compared to Adobe Photoshop

4] Discrete Strategy

- **Customer:** Restricted customers or customers who don't have many options due to situations that legally, physically, or emotionally restrict their choice.
- **Quality:** Job done worse.
- **Price:** Costs much more.
- **When to use it:** When pricing the product higher than usual would be accepted by the customer or when the customer has no means to object. *(I don't recommend this one because once those restrictions are uplifted, the customers will continue to remember the job done worse and unjustified overpriced products they bought.)*
- **Examples:**
  - Drinks sold in the airport past security checks.
  - Water bottles on a plane.
  - Soft drinks and popcorn at the cinema.

5] Sustaining Strategy

- **Customer:** Existing customers.
- **Quality:** Job done slightly (5%) better.
- **Price:** A bit (5%) cheaper.
- **When to use it:** If you already have market share. Do not pursue this if you are new to the market, as customers only consider switching to the competition when someone else does the job way (20%) better. You wouldn't be able to acquire customers who are already doing the job with some other product. But, you can continue to improve bit by bit to maintain your position in the market and keep your competition from snatching your customers.

What's your product strategy? Do you have one yet?

If you do, then you can compare it to this diagram and see where your strategy stands. If you don't have one, there is no better time to start than now.

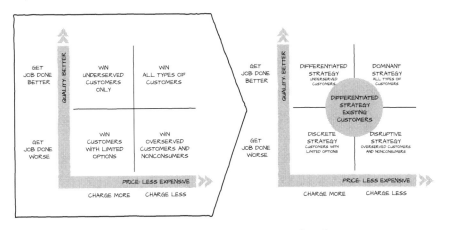

Source: Jobs-to-be-Done by Tony Ulwick

How does your customer perceive your product or service compared to other products or services she might currently be using?

- **Quality:** Does it help her get the job done better than the products or services she is currently using? Or is it worse?
- **Price:** Is it more expensive than the products or services she is currently using? Or is it less expensive?

Chapter Quiz

Congratulations on making it through Chapter 6! You should now have an in-depth understanding of your position in the market and how your product will perform based on your strategy, quality, and price.

Ready to test your knowledge with a chapter quiz?

True/False

1: You can target overserved and non-customers by offering a product that is not as good as the competition and much cheaper than what's being offered in the market. (True/False)

2: You can offer a product that does the job worse and charge more in restricted situations. (True/False)

Quiz Answer Key

Answer 1: True. If the basic job-to-be-done is achieved much cheaper, you can reach overserved customers who don't mind having less features on the product to save money and the non-customers who couldn't afford to buy the other products on the market.

Answer 2: True. Restricted customers or customers who don't have many options due to situations that legally, physically, or emotionally restrict their choice would accept paying a premium price for a lesser quality product. (For example, airport food.)

Putting It All into Action

In the previous chapter, you identified your product value proposition. Now, it's time to put it all into action and get more clarity on your pricing and quality based on your product strategy. Are you going to serve underserved or overserved customers?

Here's your checklist:
1. Decide which of the following are your target customers:
    *   Non-customers
    *   Customers with limited or no alternatives
    *   Overserved customers
    *   Underserved customers
2. Decide if your product or service will provide better or worse quality than the competition.
3. Decide if your product or service will be more or less expensive than the competition.
4. Decide on your product strategy:
    *   Differentiated Strategy
    *   Dominant Strategy
    *   Disruptive Strategy
    *   Discrete Strategy
    *   Sustaining Strategy

Now that you have finished Chapter 6, you should be clear on each product strategy and should have decided on the one that is best for your product. In Chapter 7, we'll be discussing how you're going to help your customers. We'll be working toward delivering exceptional customer experiences, so not only will they buy your product, but they will continue to buy from you again and again.

References

1. Al Ries, and Trout, Jack. Positioning the Battle for Your Mind. New York: McGraw-Hill, 2001.
2. Tony Ulwick. "The Jobs-to-Be-Done Growth Strategy Matrix." Medium. JTBD + Outcome-Driven Innovation, December 8, 2019. https://jobs-to-be-done.com/the-jobs-to-be-done-growth-strategy-matrix-426e3d5ff86e.
3. Ulwick, "The Jobs-to-Be-Done Growth Strategy Matrix," 2019.

CHAPTER 7

How Are You Going to Help
Them?

"When you have two coffee shops right next to each other, and each sells the exact same coffee at the exact same price, service design is what makes you walk into one and not the other."
-Marc Fonteijn[1]

Chapter Objectives:

- **Exceptional Customer Experience**: What happens when your customers interact with your brand?
- **Future Customer Experience**: What's your future customer's journey with your product or service?
- **Service Blueprint**: How do you design the experience with your customers, employees, and systems?

I spoke about Hello Chef in Chapter 5 *(What Problem Are You Helping Them Solve?)*, and one of the things I love about them is their personalization and customer service. It's true that I am not necessarily their ideal customer, but not a single time have I had an issue with them that wasn't resolved with grace and ease.

I remember when my very first box was delivered. I was so excited! I opened the box and found a welcoming handwritten note from Olivia, the founder of Hello Chef.. I got a cooking apron as a gift too.

Thank you for subscribing to our service. We hope you'll enjoy the cooking ahead. It's great to have you on board.

Bon Appetit?

Olivia

Hello Chef!

The note read:

Dear Sherwette,

Thank you for subscribing to our service. We hope you'll enjoy the cooking ahead. It's great to have you on board.

Bon Appetit!

Olivia ❤

Some weeks I would get random gifts like a wooden cooking spoon, a timer, or a collection of coffee capsules to try. That was a sweet touch and added to the personalization of my experience with the brand.

Psychology Tip:

Getting something for free always adds value and makes you want to give back.

I really loved the idea that I didn't have to plan meals and buy all the ingredients required to cook a restaurant-quality dish at home. I loved saving time. But I wouldn't have bought from Hello Chef again had their customer service sucked. Their customer service is one of the best I have ever encountered.

You see, the business model of Hello Chef is built on a subscription basis that automatically deducts from your credit card. Each week, you choose four recipes for at least two people, and they deliver to your doorstep with step-by-step by-the-minute recipes. And because making high-quality dishes are a bit too much for me, I order Hello Chef every once in a while when I want to indulge in a cooking week.

And so, I usually choose to "skip" weeks so that my credit card won't be charged. But sometimes, all the weeks that I skipped in advance go by, and I forget to skip another week, so my credit card gets charged with a week's worth of recipes that I didn't want. The first time this happened, I became extremely irritated until I reached out to customer care on their live chat, and they refunded my money immediately. No hassle, no questions asked. No arguments, no explanations, and no fighting. All I had to say was that it charged my credit card and that I didn't want to order that week.

That's not to say that Hello Chef could easily solve this problem by giving me the option to skip weeks until they are told otherwise. That would be a more straightforward solution. However, that said, it's worth pointing out that their customer service is on point.

When you do order a week's worth of recipes, you have to plan in advance and be sure to choose your recipes about a week prior to the delivery date. I always get a text reminding me to choose my recipes and another text reminding me when my box will be delivered.

As we discussed in Chapter 6, quality and price have a significant influence on a customer's decision to make a purchase. But the customer experience before, during, and after a purchase can be the determining factor as to whether the customer will buy again.

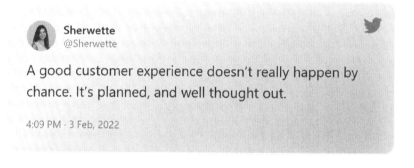

Sherwette
@Sherwette

A good customer experience doesn't really happen by chance. It's planned, and well thought out.

4:09 PM · 3 Feb, 2022

Exceptional Customer Experience: *What happens when your customers interact with your brand?*

Delivering an exceptional customer experience all comes down to little details that the customer has when interacting with your brand, so you want to ensure you focus on two things:

1. How the *future* customer experience will look.
2. How you are going to deliver the services that will ensure the future customer experience.

Place yourself in the mindset of your customer. Think about all the little details that your customer encounters when interacting with your product.
   - How will she know about your product?
   - What does she see on your website?
   - How does she order?
   - Can she pay with her preferred method of payment? Did she get confirmation after paying?
   - Will it be delivered, or will she pick it up?
   - Can she track her delivery?
   - Can she cancel her order? Change the order after she placed it?
   - Where else can she buy it?
   - What does the delivery package look like? Is it easy to open? Is it enticing to look at?
   - Wait. How about this unboxing experience? Is it "YouTube-able?"

- Now that it's open, can she use it right away? Does she have to prepare it?
- Will she have to charge your product? Can she use it if it's charging?
- Does she need to buy something else with it like a cable or battery?
- Oh no, now she's confused. Will she receive help when she needs it?
- She started using it.
- Interesting. Did she use it once? Twice? Every month? Every week? Every day?
- Did you mean to have her use it every day?
- Is it lying around in her apartment?
- Or does she use it all the time?
- Does she tell others about it?
- Does it make her life better and easier?
- What if she wants to give you some suggestions? Do you listen to her?

Tip:

All the above questions apply to physical and digital products and services. Just change your perspective on how your customer is experiencing it. For example, when buying digital software, is it easy to install? How many minutes does it require to have it set up on your computer? Does it work on both Mac and PC? Is it cloud-based? And the list could go on and on …

In Chapter 4 *(What Is Stopping Them?)*, you imagined and mapped the customer journey, as it is, with your customer's current situation.

Her troubles, her struggles, her desires.

All of that is laid out in that amazing journey you visualized.

Good news. You have done your homework.

Using the value proposition canvas, for every job your customer is trying to get done, you have mapped how you can help her.

Yes!

You might not be able to solve all your customers' problems.

But ...

You know which problems you are solving and which jobs you are helping her do better, faster, and easier.

And this is where I want to introduce two types of journeys.

1] The Current Customer Journey: We covered this in Chapter 4 *(What Is Stopping Them?)*. Remember Sally? What is Sally's current experience? The current customer journey is important to understand, especially at the beginning of the process. It will help you uncover the desires, needs, jobs-to-be-done, and those burning challenges that keep your customers up at night. It helps you understand the gaps and gives you a goldmine of potential opportunities to optimize on.

2] The Future Customer Journey: The future customer journey helps you envision your customers' target experience using your product or service and everything else in between.

Future Customer Experience: *What's your future customers' journey with your product or service?*

Just like we mapped the current customer experience in Chapter 4 (*What Is Stopping Them?*), we want to map the future customer experience. So, where to begin?

The current and future customer journeys more or less include the same items, and they can be enhanced or reduced depending on the project's requirements. However, the purpose of each of these journeys is entirely different.

The current state journey describes how customers experience the current product or service. It is used mainly to find and communicate gaps and identify opportunities for improvement. Future state journeys, on the other hand, describe how customers can potentially have a different experience. This is where the sky is the limit, and we aim to enhance the customer experience to make it optimal. It helps to imagine and experiment with a potential future experience and figure out specific steps to be tested or prototyped. *(Refer to Chapter 8: Are You Really Helping Them?)*

Let's look at the below table for simplicity:

Current vs. Future Customer Journey

	Current Customer Journey	Future Customer Journey
1. **The Main Actor, Your Persona:** The main actor representing a segment of your customers	✓	✓
2. **Journey Stages:** A group of customer steps that represent a high-level stage of your persona's experience	✓	✓
3. **Journey Steps:** Your persona's interactions to get a specific product or service	✓	✓
4. **Story:** The narrative of the journey	✓	✓
5. **Touchpoints:** The steps your persona interacts directly with your brand	✓	✓
6. **Moments of Truth:** Moments that make or break your relationship with your persona	✓	✓
7. **Jobs-to-be-Done:** Actions your persona is trying to get done	✓	✓
8. **Challenges:** Problems your persona is facing	✓	
9. **Delights:** Moments that make your persona happier	✓	✓
10. **Emotions:** The feeling your persona is experience during a specific step	✓	✓
11. **Products or Services:** Your product or service	✓	✓
12. **Channels:** Methods your personas interacts with you	✓	✓
13. **Tools:** Tools your persona is using to get a job done	✓	✓
14. **Improvement Opportunities:** Opportunities that can improve your persona's experience	✓	✓

Tip:

Refer to Chapter 4 (What Is Stopping Them?) for descriptions.

How detailed shall your customer journey be?

Depending on the purpose of your project, you may have a detailed or a very high-level customer journey. For example, if you want to research and deep-dive into customer pain points, then a detailed customer journey may make sense, such as the customer journey when booking a movie ticket. If, however, you want to help a customer throughout a larger span of her life, for example, in retirement planning or wealth management, then you want to scale up and go high-level to cover the journey throughout her lifecycle, including getting married, having children, moving countries, changing jobs, etc.

Example of journey steps for Hello Chef case study:

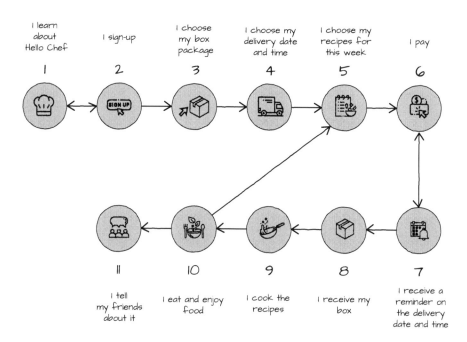

Note: The details of the journey steps for Hello Chef are hypothetical and may or may not be the actual journey that takes place. It's used for illustrative purposes only.

Service Blueprint: *How do you design the experience with your customers, employees, and systems?*

You could think of a service blueprint as an extension to the customer journey, or rather, zooming in on each of the services offered throughout the customer journey with more emphasis on *how* you will help your customer.

The service blueprint builds on the "front stage" experience that triggers your customer to interact with you. For example, you placed an ad on Facebook, then the customer landed on your website and started chatting with you via the live chat option.

The service blueprint details other layers that include a comprehensive view of how your physical/digital products, staff, automation tools, and support processes work together to deliver an exceptional customer experience.

A service blueprint typically includes the following lanes, and it may be expanded, reduced, and modified, again, based on the project's purpose.

1. **Physical/Digital Evidences:** Anything your customer interacts with you through, be it your office, service center, website, email, SMS, chatbot, phone, printed manual, or even your packaging.
2. **Customer Actions:** Those are usually the customer journey steps you have already depicted in the customer journey.

3. **Line of Interaction:** Divides customer interactions with frontstage actions.

4. **Frontstage Actions:** The activities of frontline employees, such as answering inquiries in the live chat platform.

5. **Line of Visibility:** Divides actions that are done by frontstage and backstage employees.

6. **Backstage Actions:** The activities of back-end employees, such as initiating shipment or assigning a ticket to a second level or external support. Customers do not interact with employees who perform backstage actions.

7. **Internal Interaction:** Divides actions between backstage and support processes and other internal departments.

8. **Support Processes:** Those are processes that are set up as a foundation for the service. For example, automated billing or automated account activation post-payment.

If we take the example of Hello Chef, we could visualize the service blueprint as follows:

Hello Chef Service Blueprint (1/3)

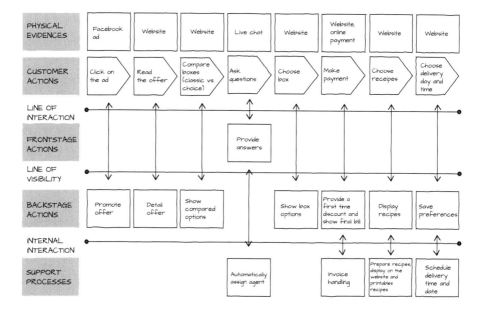

Hello Chef Service Blueprint (2/3)

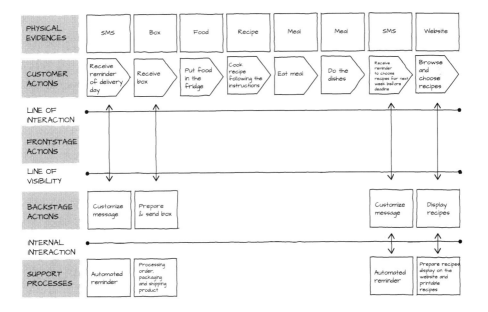

Hello Chef Service Blueprint (3/3)

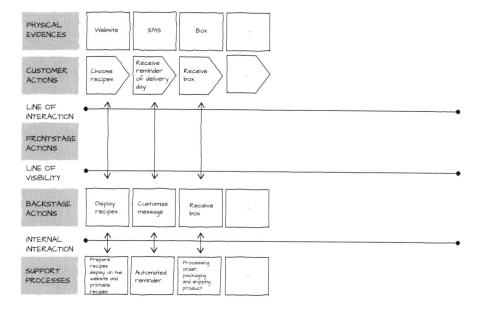

Note: The details of the service blueprint for Hello Chef are hypothetical and may or may not be the actual process that takes place. It's used for illustrative purposes only.

You see, for every action that the customer goes through, there are multiple actions and support processes that happen on the back end. The customer can only feel the engagement with the brand through the "physical evidences" and the "frontstage actions." That, however, doesn't mean that the backstage actions, internal interactions, and support processes are not as important. On the contrary, if the services offered to customers are well designed with the customer at heart, no matter how exceptional your website is, or how well trained your frontstage employees are, your customers may end up with a not-so-pleasant experience.

Chapter Quiz

So, you have come to the end of Chapter 7. Great job on getting so far through this book! And, at this point, you should be well on your way to designing great experiences for your customers so not only will they love your product, but they will love every interaction with your brand.

Are you ready for the chapter quiz? Give it a try!

True/False

1: The future customer experience Journey Map helps you identify the pain points your customers will go through. (True/False)

2: The service blueprint details how your products and services will deliver an exceptional customer experience. (True/False)

Quiz Answer Key

Answer 1: False. The future customer experience Journey Map helps you envision how your product or service will help your customers. The current customer Journey Map helps identify the pain points.

Answer 2: True. The service blueprint details how your products and services will deliver an exceptional customer experience by depicting the frontline and backstage employees' actions, internal interactions, and support processes.

Putting It All into Action

I am sure you've started to think about your customers' future experience, so it's time to put it all into action.

Here's your checklist:

1. Map your customer's future experience.
2. Design the service blueprint for each of the services or products that you offer to your customers.

Now that you have finished Chapter 7, you should be ready to map out your customers' future experiences and design your services to deliver this experience. In Chapter 8, we'll be discussing how to know if your product or service is really helping your customers and when it's time to re-evaluate and go back to the drawing board.

References

1. Marc Fonteijn. "What Is Service Design: The Final Answer." Service Design Show, July 28, 2020. https://www.servicedesignshow.com/what-is-service-design/.

CHAPTER 8

Are You Really Helping Them?

"Any product that needs a manual to work is broken."
-Elon Musk

Chapter Objectives:

- **Testing Products and Services**: What to test?
- **Product or Service Demand**: Is there a demand for your product?
- **Product or Service Usability or Functionality**: Do your customers "get" it and know how to use it?
- **Handling Feedback**: How do you handle feedback, and what do you do with it?

Ideas are great until they are proven not to be.

Sometimes, things are so clear in our heads, but when our customers see them, they have no clue what the heck we are talking about.

One of the projects I worked on in my consulting career involved building the strategy and core structure of a brand and product for one of our clients. We were also the ones implementing it and bringing it to life. The project, in fact, was very exciting, and we thought about many things I mentioned here in this book, such as customer research, challenges, jobs, a new product, product fit, and the new awesome customer experience that would be delivered to our customers. Part of the experience involved using a portal or a website. The end product looked extremely sleek; we worked with one of the top software houses in the world.

It was so exciting. We were working with world-class branding agencies, developers, and consultants.

And then the time came to test our fantastic new product. We reached out to a selection of target customers and gave them a few test cases to explore our digital product.

Awesome products don't need explanations, right?

As Elon Musk, says *"Any product that needs a manual to work is broken."*

But, our customers were confused. They didn't get it. They didn't see the point of our product, nor did they express any interest in using it.

That was a bit of a shocker. We had worked so hard, not to mention the amount of money we spent on that product.

We took the feedback, and we had to pivot. The portal was revamped entirely.

It was a bit late in the game, though. We had already built a working product and all the hard work, time, and money went straight out the window.

It was a lesson learned the hard way. It was a bit late, but not too late because we hadn't launched it to the public just yet.

Instead, prototyping the product and testing it before building it would have helped us come to the same conclusion—that no one got it—a little bit earlier. And the cost and time associated with it would have been much, much less.

As John Maeda says, *"If a picture is worth 1,000 words, a prototype is worth 1,000 meetings."*[1]

Testing Products and Services: *What to test?*

With all this research, have you done enough research?

How much research is enough?

If you doubt yourself for long and continue researching to ensure your idea is what your customers really want, you will end up stalling.

That's why you need to test it and get it over with.

Test it with your customers, though, not with yourself, not with your spouse, not with your team, and not with your friends.

Let me say it once more. Test it with your customers.

What you think is not what your customers think, and no matter how many times you decide to walk in their shoes or wear the "customer's hat," the reality is, you are not your customer.

It's time to get back to your customers.

You see, sometimes we think we come up with the best ideas, and sometimes our first ideas are the best ideas; however, sometimes that very first idea is what led to the second, third, and *then* that final, great idea.

You can create the value proposition canvas for each of your customers. You can jot down how your products and services will transform your customers in their journey to get their job done and achieve their desires.

All that might sound great, but if you don't test it, then you won't be able to understand the true potential your product or service could have on your customers.

Testing should be your way of living as a business, whether you are creating a new product, enhancing an old one, or writing copy to sell it.

If you are delivering a product or service, there are two things that you can test:

1. Product or service demand.
2. Product or service usability or functionality.

Product or Service Demand: *Is there a demand for your product?*

We discussed the value proposition in Chapter 5 *(What Problem Are You Helping Them Solve?)*, and you learned you could offer each of your customer segments products or services that will help them do their jobs better and faster, alleviate their pains, and make them happier. It's clear in your head how your products help your customers.

But how about your customers? Is it clear to them? Will they value it?

The value proposition testing or prototyping helps you get confirmation for the following questions:

- Does your product really help your customers do the jobs they want to do better, faster, and easier?
- Does your product fulfill a specific desire?
- Does it help customers overcome their challenges?
- Does it really fit into their experience and the bigger context of their everyday life?

When you are trying to test your product or service demand, you don't even have to have your product or service ready in the first place. This saves you a ton of time and money. This method is especially beneficial if you are creating a new product from scratch or want to enhance an existing one.

How do you do it?

You don't need to have your product ready to test the idea.

What you can do, though, is **test the demand** by initiating a **mini-marketing campaign** to gauge your customers' interest in that product. It could be as simple as a Facebook or Google ad. It could also be a crowdfunding campaign.

For example, if it's a new service or an information product, you can ask your customers to sign up for the waiting list to be informed once they are available. If it's a physical or a digital product, they can sign up to be one of the beta testers for that product with a generous discount to first-time users.

Do you see a pattern?

Expert Tip:

> "To get an accurate indicator of commercial viability, don't ask people if they would buy-ask them to buy. The response to the second is the only one that matters." - Timothy Ferriss[2]

There are two approaches that you can follow.
- **Approach A:** The preorder option for that specific service or product.

- **Approach B:** The "free" sign-up option to a waiting list or "free" early access to the product or service you are offering.

The two approaches have interesting psychology reflections, though **the level of interest or demand is stronger when your customers pay even as little as one dollar.**

Why?

When someone pays as little as one dollar for your product, they are more likely to pay more on another product, and that is an excellent indicator for the product demand proof that you need. You want to confirm that there are buyers out there for your product or service. More often than not, people sign up for free stuff to shop around. I know for sure I am one of those people. I am curious to know what is out there, so I sign up for the freebie without really needing the product or service ... #Guilty, I know ... Then I find myself bombarded with emails in my inbox of offers I really don't care about.

So, the moral of the story is if you want to have a vetted list of customers who would confirm demand for your product, make it cost as little as one dollar, and see how that unfolds for you.

That's not to say that offering your product or services for free doesn't come without the benefit. On the contrary, there are very interesting behavioral "obligations" embedded within your customers' mindset once they get something valuable for free.

Roger Dooley, in his book Brainfluence,[3] mentioned different studies and experiments that showcase the power of the word "free" on consumer behavior.

"To our hunter-gatherer's brain, a free item represents the proverbial low-hanging fruit. That is, a resource that can be obtained with near-zero effort." —Roger Dooley[4]

Psychology Tip:

Getting something for free that provides value activates the rule of reciprocation, which creates something similar to a "favor bank." It activates the "giving back" feeling from the receiver.

"The rule of reciprocation says that we should try to repay, in kind, what another person has provided us."
-Robert Cialdini[5]

The approach you decide to follow is up to you. However, that step is very important because it will give you the confidence to know you are working in the right direction and not just burning energy and wasting your time.

One more thing.

If a mini-marketing campaign sounds scary to you because you don't have the tools, the budget, or the time to do it, you can simply ask a selection of your target customers. This can be carried out as part of an email marketing campaign (if you have a list) or even 1:1 chats with your customers. It doesn't need to be complicated; it just needs to get done.

"You don't have to get it perfect; you just have to get it going." -Jack Canfield

Done is better than perfect.

Product or Service Usability or Functionality Testing: *Do your customers "get" it and know how to use it?*

Now that you have some clarity on your product and its value proposition, you can start designing your products. Listen, I know that's one of the hardest things to do, and a million things start running through your head.

- *I don't have the resources.*
- *I don't know how.*
- *I am not technical, and my product is digital.*
- *I don't have the right tools or team.*
- *I don't even have the money to get the help I need.*
- *How about the technical feasibility? The look and feel? The integration?*
- *How will it all work together?*

Sound familiar?

When you start thinking down that path, it becomes very dangerous because you are holding yourself back. Fear gets in the way. You get in your own way.

The good news is you don't have to get it perfect.

When you test your product, your product doesn't have to be perfect.

All you need is a **prototype**, and that prototype also doesn't need to be perfect.

First things first ... What is a prototype?

A **prototype** is a quick, rough model of your idea to help you communicate it with others, test its value proposition, find alternatives, and continuously improve it.

Your prototype is not the actual, final product or service that you would be selling. Instead, it's a mere representation of what you want your product to do. And, depending on the stage you're at in developing the product and who you're communicating it to, it can be a simple sketch on a napkin or as complex as an almost-real product that no one would suspect is not a working product.

Your product "maturity" will help you determine your prototype fidelity level.

What is prototype fidelity?

Your **prototype fidelity** is how refined it is and how it conveys the look and feel of the final product. It varies based on visual design, content, and interactivity. A high-fidelity prototype looks like a real product, and in some cases, you won't be able to differentiate whether it's real or not. Low-fidelity prototypes are quick and easy and could be as simple as a sketch on a napkin.

You can have low-fidelity or high-fidelity prototypes, depending on what stage you are at.

To do so, think of the following questions:
- How much detail does it include?
- What resolution does it have?
- How much time and effort are you putting into it?

When you are starting out, it's best to start with low-fidelity prototypes. Then, as your product becomes more mature and grows toward implementation, you can increase the fidelity of your prototype.

The goal here is to get feedback quickly, without spending too much time or effort on the idea when it needs to be tested.

Let's take, for example, digital products, where:
- **Low fidelity** prototypes can be as simple as an idea sketch, even on a napkin.
- **Medium fidelity** could be wireframes or **clickable prototypes.**
- **High fidelity** could be a functional **proof of concept** product with **throwaway code** or even a **beta version** of the digital product.

Low fidelity prototypes give you the advantage of communicating your ideas fast. But fast isn't always meaningful. Depending on the audience and purpose of the prototype, you will have to take a step back and evaluate a mindful fidelity level that will get you the most helpful feedback. You have to find the sweet spot between fast and meaningful and slowly move from a low fidelity to a higher one—as you need it, when you need it.

- **Clickable Prototype**: A visual representation of the end product that offers an interactive experience similar to the final working product. Unlike static wireframes, clickable prototypes show several states of the website or application. Users can navigate different buttons and pages and even use mock-up drop-down lists to make different selections.

- **Proof of Concept**: An exercise that provides results that a business idea is viable, feasible, and can be turned into a reality. Usually, it is required to convince specific stakeholders, such as investors, to support an idea or a product.

- **Throwaway code**: A piece of code created to prototype a concept as a proof of concept that is rewritten properly once the idea is approved. It's a quick and dirty method to show a near-real product to the desired audience without spending so much time developing it. Throwaway code is meant for prototyping and not for the actual end product.

- **Beta version**: A piece of software that can be tested by users outside the company that developed it before it goes to general release. It could be tested with dummy data to test product usability and functionality. Unlike throwaway code, beta products are continuously enhanced with a small group of users. A beta release usually has bugs, so

> users' expectations are adjusted from a reliability and quality standpoint.
> - **Pilot:** A pilot is similar to the beta release, however, with one difference: the product is final, and the data being tested is real. A pilot is eventually released to the general population in a pilot format.

When working with a new product, don't underestimate the power of a prototype, even as a sketch or made of cardboard. If it's a digital product, a simple clickable prototype will tell a story that endless slideshows could never describe. No presentations, just the actual product in its very early stages. A prototype creates a different kind of energy because each person involved, whether internal or external, gets to not only imagine how it will look or how it will function but actually see it for themselves. Prototypes create passion and ownership within the team—and those on their own are enough reasons to build prototypes.

> *"The best prototype is one that, in the simplest and most efficient way, makes the possibilities and limitations of a design idea visible and measurable."* -Lim, Stolterman and Tenenberg[6]

What if you were thinking, *"Sounds great, but my product is not actually a digital product."*

The good news is that both low- and high-fidelity concepts apply to all different sorts of products, including physical products, digital products, AND experience or service products, which is what we are going to be discussing next.

But before we do, remember that testing and prototyping are ongoing processes. Get it done. Not perfect. But done. You test it. Make it better. Still not perfect. You test it again. Make it better again. You test it once more ... You get the idea.

Even when you go live and you are no longer in a pilot or a beta testing phase, continue testing to get feedback and make it better.

When it comes to testing, there is no one-size-fits-all. It all depends on what product you are designing and delivering to your customers. You might be thinking, *"What kind of prototype should I be doing?"* and that's alright.

The one thing you want to always keep in mind is that it's **better to start with a low fidelity prototype to test.**

Before going any further on the different types of prototypes, **let me ask you one thing:**

What kind of product are you offering? Is it …

1. A physical product?
2. A digital product?
3. An experience or service?

Based on the type of product you are offering, you can select what prototype you want to start with.

Regardless of your product type, there are a few things to ask yourself when deciding on your prototype fidelity level:

1. Is the initial idea communicated?
2. Is everyone aligned on what the product will look like? Are the brains of your company in sync with what you want to offer?
3. How much time do you have to create it?
4. Do you have the expertise to create it?
5. Should it feel real?
6. Should it give the illusion that it is a working product?
7. Is it close to production?
8. What budget do you have?

After answering these questions, you will have a better idea of your prototype fidelity. How you choose to conduct experience prototypes is up to you, your budget, and your resources.

<u>Physical Products:</u>

What are the different prototype options for physical products?
- Sketching
- Paper or cardboard mock-up (doesn't apply to all products)
- 3D printing (doesn't apply to all products)
- Handmade with real materials
- Small scale production (Go-Live)
- Scalable mass production (Go-Live)

Physical Products:

Prototype	Fidelity	Ease	Time	Feels Real	Requires Specialist Expertise
Sketching	Low	Easy	Quickest	Not really	Not really
Paper or Cardboard Mock-Up (doesn't apply to all products)	Low	Easy	Quick	Not really	Not really
3D Print (doesn't apply to all products)	Medium	Easy	Quick	Yes!	Yes!
Handmade with Real Materials	Medium	Medium-Easy	Takes more time to create	Yes!	Yes!
Small Scale Production (Go-Live)	High	Medium	Takes even more time to create	It's real! *(Small scale)*	Yes!
Scalable Mass Production (Go-Live)	It's happening! Your product is real!	Medium-Hard	Takes even more time to create	It's real!	Yes!

, Note: Numerous resources can help you learn more about the different prototype approaches. One of my favorites is *"This is Service Design"*[7]. I highly recommend it if you would like to know more details about those approaches or if you want to dig deeper into service design.

The fact that those prototype approaches are listed above for physical products doesn't mean you have to test each type of prototype or create one.

Choose what best works for you and your product.

Case Study: Hair Addict Product - The Indian Recipe

Remember *The Indian Recipe* I talked about in Chapter 2? *(What Do They Want to Do?)*

The Indian Recipe is a perfect example of a physical product that was tested and proved to be working and in high demand before being mass produced.

Let's take a moment and think—what kind of prototype best fits this product?

If we look at the physical prototype options right away, we know that sketching, a paper mock-up, and 3D printing are far from relevant to *The Indian Recipe* simply because it doesn't apply.

What does?

The **handmade prototype** makes more sense. In fact, The *Indian Recipe* was readily available to *The Hair Addict*'s potential customers in the Facebook group, where many people were buying the ingredients and making the recipe themselves.

Just because I kind of failed at it doesn't mean everyone else did too. Actually, many prepared the recipe themselves and were seeing incredible results.

Today, the product is readily available for purchase on the general market, to buy and apply right away, with plans to cross borders and become an international product for the masses to use and enjoy longer, healthier hair.

Digital Products

Some could categorize digital products as the hottest category. Many startups that turn into multi-million dollar—if not multi-billion dollar—businesses are digital products. Think Facebook, Paypal, etc.

And even though a digital product doesn't come with manufacturing costs, it does come with a lot of expenses to develop, test, debug, and develop again.

So, it's essential to test the product, how your customers are using it, and if it serves their needs, jobs, wants, and challenges. One major study of digital products is usability, where a lot of psychology on how users interact with your product is considered.

What is usability?

In simple words, **usability** is how easy it is to use an interactive device, system, or website.

When you decide to design a product, you are trying to solve your customer's problem. You want to provide your customer with a functional product that is easy to use, and therefore useful.

Ignore this and you will have trouble getting people to "use" your product, whether it's a website, a mobile app, a system, or a device.

Why is usability testing important?

Designers are usually attached to their designs, so usability testing is conducted to gather feedback from a set of real users who are the target segment for that particular product.

Usability testing is conducted to measure the usability of that product to those real users.

What should we test? What are we trying to measure in usability?

Whitney Quesenbery outlined five usability dimensions to help measure the level of usability of a particular design,[8] and I added a sixth one, "memorability."

1. **Learnability:** How easy is it to learn your way around the new system? Did the user require external help? Did he have to look through a manual?
2. **Efficiency:** How long did it take you to perform a task? Seconds? Minutes? Hours? The whole day trying to figure it out?
3. **Effective:** How easy was it to carry out the task accurately? Were you able to complete the task?
4. **Error Tolerant:** How many mistakes did you make while performing the task? Were you able to fix it right away, or did you have to do the whole thing all over again from the start?

5. **Engaging and Satisfying:** Did you enjoy performing the task? Was it a pleasurable experience, or did you dread doing it?

6. **Memorability:** How easy is it to remember how to perform the task after not doing it for a while?

How many usability tests are enough?

According to Jakob Nielsen, PhD, user advocate and principal of the Nielsen Norman Group, which he co-founded with Dr. Donald A. Norman, **five usability tests**[9] with real users is sufficient.

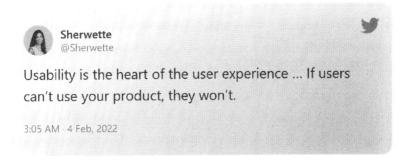

> **Sherwette**
> @Sherwette
>
> Usability is the heart of the user experience ... If users can't use your product, they won't.
>
> 3:05 AM · 4 Feb, 2022

What are the different prototype options for digital products?

- Sketching
- Wireframes
- Paper prototype
- Interactive clickable prototype
- Functional proof of concept using throwaway code in a testing environment
- Functional beta version or a pilot on an actual production environment (Go-Live)
- Fully functional and integrated product in production environment (Go-Live)

So, which prototype are you going to test for your product?

Digital Products:

Prototype	Fidelity	Ease	Time	Feels Real	Requires Specialist Expertise
Sketching	Low	Easy	Quickest	Not really	Not really
Wireframes	Low	Easy	Quick	Not really	Not really
Paper Prototype	Medium	Easy	Quick	Yes!	Not really
Interactive Clickable Prototype	Medium	Medium-Easy	Takes more time to create	Yes!	Yes!
Functional Proof of Concept Using Throwaway Code in Testing Environment	High	Medium	Takes even more time to create	Feels so real	Yes!
Functional Beta Version or a Pilot on Actual Production Environment (Go-Live)	High	Medium	Takes even more time to create	It's real! *(Small scale)*	Yes!
Fully Functional and Integrated Product in Production Environment (Go-Live)	It's happening! Your product is real!	Medium-Hard	Takes even more time to create	It's real!	Yes!

Experience or Service Products:

Delivering an experience or a service can be tricky. Here, you are not delivering a physical product, nor are you delivering a digital one.

When you are delivering an experience and want to test it, you have two options:

1. Develop a mock-up environment where your customers can go through the "prototyped" experience and "experience it for themselves."
2. Conduct a prototype where customers can "imagine" what it feels like to experience something. This can help them think through the process and its logic and sympathize with the different interactions to find any gaps. This could be delivered using tools, such as storytelling and Journey Maps *(Refer to Chapter 4: What Is Stopping Them? & Chapter 7: How Are You Helping Them?)*

What are the different prototype options for experiences and services?
- Sketching
- Storyboard and storytelling
- Investigative rehearsal
- Pilot Go-Live
- Rollout Go-Live

Investigative Rehearsal: A prototyping technique involving role-playing with actors to model human interaction and empathize with the customer and employee experience.

Experience or Service Products:

Prototype	Fidelity	Ease	Time	Feels Real	Requires Specialist Expertise
Sketching	Low	Easy	Quickest	Not real	Not really
Storyboard and Storytelling	Low	Easy	Quick	Not real	Not really
Investigative Rehearsal	Medium	Easy	Quick	Not real	Not really
Pilot Go-Live	High	Medium	Takes even more time to create	It's real! *(Small scale)*	Yes!
Rollout Go-Live	It's happening! Your product is real!	Medium-Hard	Takes even more time to create	It's real!	Yes!

Now that we went through the different prototype options based on your product type ...

Did you notice anything in common among them?

Sketching is the constant prototype for each of the product types.

Why?

It's easy and quick to produce, not to mention practical; all you need is a pen and paper or a whiteboard. As we draw, we can communicate our ideas more fluently and get feedback on whether they make sense in the first place.

Handling Feedback: *How do you handle feedback, and what do you do with it?*

When you get feedback, it could be either GOOD or BAD. When it's good, your ego is satisfied, and you are happy. So you think to yourself, *"Good job. I am on the right path."*

But ...

When the feedback is mainly critique, it may discourage you. You could feel like you have wasted your efforts and your ideas are not any good ... and if you think that way, let me stop you right there and tell you, a failed prototype is not a failure. On the contrary, a failed prototype is a win.

Wait, what?

Yes, read that again. A failed prototype is a win. You put so much thought and effort into it so it seems like a total loss, but it's moments like these that are crucial to your success.

You've spent all this time researching, ideating, working on those value propositions. You've learned what didn't work, and you will go back to the drawing board, add more challenges that you weren't aware of, refine the jobs-to-be-done, and perhaps revisit those emotional desires that you thought were driving your customers to do those jobs, but in reality, they weren't.

Okay, now that we got that out of the way. Let's be honest—some people could have hurtful comments, and that's OKAY.

One of the following of many possible comments that you might hear could be:
- "Is that it?"
- "Is this really how it will look?"
- "Can we see more options?"

You just need to continue emphasizing that *"This is just a prototype"* and that *"Your feedback is valuable, and we want to hear more of it."*

Remind them that there will be other versions of the prototype that you will bring for testing, considering their feedback, and with enhancements.

Okay, so you got all of this feedback in the prototype session.

What do you do with it?
1. First, put all the new ideas on an idea wall or digital wall, whatever works for you.
2. Prioritize and categorize them based on your personas, the jobs they are doing, their pains, and their gains. Then, think about which ones you can incorporate and which will provide the most value to your customers.
3. Revisit your research artifacts, including your personas, their desires, customer journeys, jobs-to-be-done, and your value proposition.
4. Visualize it. See how it fits into your understanding and your ideation process. Perhaps even have a research wall on which

you lay out all those artifacts, and put the new insights on top of them. Sticky notes work, too; you don't need anything fancy. There are digital tools that could help you do that as well.

5. Pivot, prototype, and test again.

The important part is to take the feedback and **DO something with it**. Think, **"How can I make my product better to serve my customer needs?"**

Tip:

Prototyping and testing is an iterative process. It's not necessarily a one-time activity that you do before you go live or right before you launch your product. However, it's an extremely powerful tool, and you can use it for multiple purposes such as:

1. **Exploring new ideas.** What do customers really want?

2. **Evaluating the designed product.** Will my customers like or use what I just built for them?

3. **Communicating and presenting it.** Will my customers, wider team, and investors understand what in the world I am trying to build here?

Chapter Quiz

Congratulations on making it through Chapter 8! Did you start thinking about which method you are going to use to test your product yet?

And, it's that time again! Ready for a chapter quiz?

True/False

1: You have to spend a lot of money creating a prototype close to the "real" product to get customer feedback. (True/False)

2: Experiences or services cannot be tested and need to be implemented to see actual results with real people. (True/False)

Quiz Answer Key

Answer 1: False. Testing can start with low-fidelity prototypes that don't cost a lot of money or time, such as idea sketches, paper mock-ups, or early-stage clickable wireframes.

Answer 2: False. Experiences can be tested by:

- Developing a mock-up environment where your customers can go through the "prototyped" experience and "experience it for themselves."
- Conducting a prototype where customers can "imagine" what it's like to experience something. This can help them think through the process and its logic and sympathize with the different interactions to find any gaps. This could be delivered using tools such as storytelling and Journey Maps.

Putting It All into Action

In the previous chapters, you worked on your product's value proposition and designed your customers' future experience. Now, it's time to test it out and put it all into action.

Here's your checklist:

1. Decide whether you are testing the product demand or usability.
2. Product demand testing:
   - Decide whether you are testing product demand by offering it for free or by charging a discounted price for early signups.
3. Product usability or functionality testing:
   - Is your product a physical, digital, or experience product?
   - Answer the following questions to decide the fidelity level of your prototype:
     - Is the initial idea communicated?
     - Is everyone aligned with what the product will look like? Are the brains of your company in sync with what you want to offer?
     - How much time do you have to create it?
     - Do you have the expertise to create it?
     - Should it feel real?
     - Should it give the illusion that it is a working product?
     - Is it close to production?
     - What budget do you have?

4. Test it, revisit it, then test it again.

You have come so far! And you've learned so much about your customers, as well as ideated and tested your product innovations with your customers. Well done. Now, it's time to make sure that they know about your products and services. In Chapter 9, we will be talking about your customers' awareness and their previous experiences with your product(s), and how to get your customer's attention so that they actually *buy*. So, keep reading!

References

1. John Maeda. "'If a Picture Is Worth 1000 Words, a Prototype Is Worth 1000 Meetings.' -Saying at @Ideo." Twitter. Twitter, October 5, 2014. https://twitter.com/johnmaeda/status/518556402902925313?lang=en.

2. Timothy Ferriss. *The 4-Hour Workweek: Escape 9-5, Live Anywhere, and Join the New Rich*. New York: Harmony Books, 2012.

3. Roger Dooley. "Brainfluence." Roger Dooley, July 22, 2021. https://www.rogerdooley.com/books/brainfluence/.

4. Dooley, "Brainfluence," 2021.

5. Robert B. Cialdini. *Influence: Science and Practice*. Harlow, Essex: Pearson, 2014.

6. Youn-Kyung Lim, Stolterman, Erik, and Tenenberg, Josh. "The Anatomy of Prototypes." ACM Transactions on Computer-Human Interaction 15, no. 2 (2008): 1–27. https://dl.acm.org/doi/10.1145/1375761.1375762.

7. Mark Stickdorn, and Schneider, Jakob. *This Is Service Design Thinking: Basics - Tools - Cases*. 1st ed. Amsterdam: BIS Publishers, 2010.

8. Whitney Quesenbery. Twitter. Twitter, 2003. https://twitter.com/whitneyq.

9. Jakob Nielsen. "Why You Only Need to Test with 5 Users." Nielsen Norman Group, March 18, 2000. https://www.nngroup.com/articles/why-you-only-need-to-test-with-5-users/.

CHAPTER 9

Do They Know about
Your Product?

"What really decides consumers to buy or not to buy is the content of your advertising, not its form."
-David Ogilvy

Chapter Objectives:

- **Desire**: Why do customers buy?
- **Your Message**: How are you crafting your message?
- **Your Headline**: How are you getting your customer's attention?
- **Your Copy Strategy**: How are you building up your customer's interest to buy?

I moved to a new apartment again in 2021. While moving all my furniture in the apartment, along with my new plants and my very own paintings (which, by the way, I painted in the previous new apartment, thanks to having ample space), I felt that my furniture was a bit old. It had been seven years since I had moved to Dubai, and I had bought the cheapest furniture possible from IKEA. I didn't have the money at the time to invest in good furniture. I thought to myself, *I want a new couch, desk, and chair, and I will just get rid of the ones I have right now.*

I know I can try my best to create mood boards, browse stores and the internet to find something I would like to have in my space. But, I also know that I am not an interior designer. Yes, some part of me is an artist as I love painting. Yes, I am a creative person, and I'd like to think that I have good taste. But, I am not an interior designer. I always thought that when the time came for me to finally buy my own apartment, I would want to hire an interior designer to make my space beautiful.

The thought I had in the back of my head was that interior designers charge big bucks. That is, until one day I was browsing the internet for ideas on how to make my new home more beautiful, and I stumbled upon a company called Moodfit[1] via an Instagram advertisement.

With Moodfit, I would choose the room in my apartment that I wanted to redecorate or design from scratch, answer a few questions so they would know my taste, and when I was finished with all that, it was time to pay. Like most people, I abandoned the cart. I didn't know a thing about this company. A few days later, I received a call from them, and it was in the middle of my moving day, so I asked them to call again in a few days.

I spoke with a lovely woman. Her name was Christelle, and she explained the whole process to me. As I already had my own furniture, paintings, and plants, all I needed was a few tweaks to make my living room a little cozier. All I had to pay was 99 USD with a discount that I was given for my birthday, which was only a couple of days away. I would give the designer the floor plan, all the inspirations, pictures that I liked, and my current furniture and decorative materials. The designer would understand my budget and taste, then help me with my vision for that living room and either tell me where I could go buy the items, or they could buy, deliver, and assemble the items for me, all of which, of course, came with additional cost.

I checked their website, and although it wasn't the top-notch designer work you would expect, it was actually pretty decent, and I thought of signing up with them. Because, at the end of the day, I am not an interior designer. And I felt that I couldn't afford one at that specific time in my life. Even if I could have afforded it, I didn't want to spend that much on an apartment that I would likely move out of after a year or two.

So, what made me consider using Moodfit's services?

I started imagining what it would look like for me.

Desire: *Why do customers buy?*

"A picture is worth a thousand words."

Why is that? Why is a picture worth a thousand words?

A picture makes it easy for you to imagine. It helps you "see" what you are supposed to imagine, and so it's worth a thousand words.

Think about it.

Before you decide to buy a new product, you first need to see yourself using it, just like when I started imagining "hiring" Moodfit to help me revamp my living room.

Have you ever found yourself saying:
  - "I just can't see myself living here?"
  - "I can't see myself eating THAT?"
  - "I can't see myself wearing this?"
  - "I'll believe it when I see it."

When you can't imagine yourself doing something or using something, you simply don't buy it.

Imagining yourself using a product is how desire is born.

Phil M. Jones, in his book *"Exactly What to Say,"*[2] put it nicely.

"If you cannot see yourself doing something, the chances of you doing it are slim to none. People make decisions based on the images they see in their minds, so if you can place pictures in people's minds, then you can use the results of those images to influence their decisions."
--Phil M Jones

I am sure you have spent a lot of time and effort crafting your product. You have brainstormed and worked with your team to develop new, innovative, and creative solutions to real customer problems. You have worked day and night. You did all of that.

Yet, when it comes to explaining this product, you have worked so hard for your customers, maybe you stumbled a little; then you thought you nailed it, and you went and tested it out with someone you know or even one of your customers, only to find out that they didn't understand a thing you were talking about.

At the end of the day, you are not a copywriter. That's not your craft. Your craft is the expertise you have in building up that product.

You put your product on your website, and no one is clicking the "Add to Cart" button. You spend money on ads, and still, no one is clicking.

"What went wrong?" you ask yourself.

You do more research. You read about copywriting, and everyone tells you, *"Hey, stop writing about the features of your product and start writing about its benefits."*

You do that ... Things get slightly better, but not a whole lot.

You want to engage your customers. You want to attract those quality clients that you have spent your days, nights, and weekends crafting this amazing product to serve.

Yes, it's great to know the benefits. It's incredibly impressive, but that's not why customers buy. That's not why YOU buy anything.

Do you want to know why customers buy?

Customers buy their hopes, dreams, fears, and desires. **Customers buy their desires.**

They don't buy the "benefit" of a soft couch. They buy the comfort it brings. They buy the intimacy they imagine they will have with their loved ones.

Customers don't buy expensive Starbucks coffee because of its premium quality. They buy it because it makes them feel good about themselves. They buy treats. They buy how it makes them feel.

And just like Harvard marketing professor Theodore Levitt said, *"People don't want to buy a quarter-inch drill. They want a quarter-inch hole. But in fact, people rarely want a hole in the wall either; they want a comfortable living room."*

That's what you want to tap into with your content to reach the hearts of your customers and make them tremble, reaching for that "Add to Cart," "Buy Now," or whatever other call to action button you have.

Customers don't buy "nice-to-haves." They buy their own fulfillment. They buy their happiness.

Your Message: *How are you crafting your message?*

Simply tap into your customers' desires and place them into your message. Think of your content (advertisements, product descriptions, videos, blogs, etc.) as the bridge that will connect your customers' desires, hopes, dreams, and fears with your product.

You can't create new desires; you can only direct your customers' desires to your products.

> *"Copy cannot create desire for a product. It can only take the hopes, dreams, fears, and desires that already exist in the hearts of millions of people and focus those already existing desires onto a particular product. This is the copywriter's task: not to create this mass desire-but to channel and direct it."* -Eugene Schwartz[3]

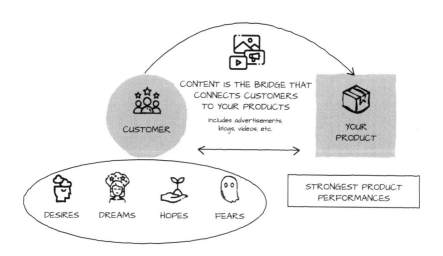

You see, there are many desires your customer has, but you don't need to tap into all of them. **You only want to touch upon the strongest desires your product performances can fulfill.** The ones your product doesn't satisfy, you don't even need to mention them.

Copy is **the bridge that will channel your customers' desires into your products.**

... But before they hit the "Add to Cart" or "Buy Now" button, your customers need to:

1. Have a burning desire.
2. Be aware of the product and identify that it does fulfill the desire they have.
3. Believe that your product will fulfill their desire without any disappointments.

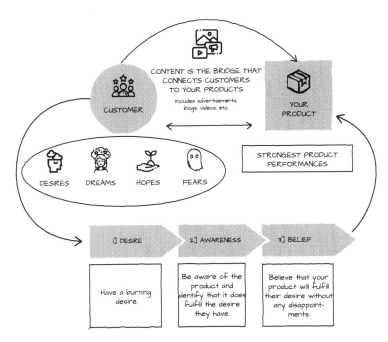

1] Desire

Let's refresh a bit on **what desire is.**

"We can define this Mass Desire quite simply. It is the public spread of a private want." —Eugene Schwartz[4]

As discussed in Chapter 3 of this book *(Why Do They Want to Do It?)*, your customers may have many desires based on the eight biological triggers.

And, there are three dimensions of desire mentioned by Eugene M. Schwartz in his book, *Breakthrough Advertising.*[5] To focus on the desires that would make your customer happiest and help you increase your profits, you should examine these three dimensions. Once you do, you will be able to prioritize which ones you are going to tackle in your messaging:

1. **Urgency, intensity, and degree of demand to be satisfied.** *How often does your customer get this urge?* Think constant migraine vs. minor headache.
2. **Staying power, degree of repetition, and the inability to be satiated.** *How badly does your customer want that desire to be satisfied?* Think raw hunger vs. craving a gourmet meal.
3. **Scope – the number of people who share this desire.** *How many people have this desire?* Think the number of people who would buy a quality durable product vs. those who don't mind paying for repairs or buying a new version every now and then.

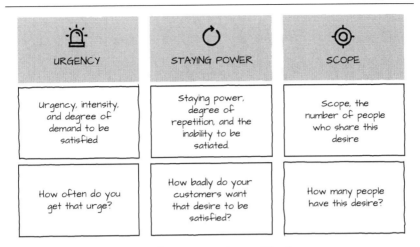

The Three Dimensions of Desire

(Refer to Chapter 3: Why Do They Want to Do It?)

Choose your customers' strongest desire based on its urgency, staying power, and the number of people who want the same thing.

2] Awareness

Even though you might have identified your customers' desires and prioritized them according to the three dimensions of desire, it doesn't necessarily mean that those desires are obvious to your customers. They don't yet know that they want or need, let alone know that your product will help them. Sometimes it makes sense for you to go ahead and continue investing in that desire, but then, you have to work to raise your customer's awareness.

How many times have you not wanted something until you saw it?

In June 2020, I moved to a new apartment where I would finally have a balcony. I made this move after the COVID-19 quarantine, where I was cramped in my small studio apartment with no balcony and not even a window that opened. Fresh air was a luxury I didn't have. So, being excited about having a bigger apartment with a balcony, I wanted to get myself a couple of outdoor chairs and a small table. That's pretty standard, and that was my ambition. I just wanted to enjoy the breeze.

Luckily for me, one of my best friends wanted to buy me a gift for my new apartment, which happened to be a few days before from my birthday.

She told me, *"I want to get you a swing chair for the balcony."*

I was like, *"What is that?"* And ... when I saw it, I was like, *"Definitely, YES! I want that!"*

You see, it didn't even cross my mind that I wanted that swing chair for my balcony. It wasn't until I saw it that I couldn't stop thinking about "seeing" myself sitting in that swing chair on my balcony, enjoying the breeze and the incredible view from my apartment.

The moment I envisioned myself sitting in that chair and enjoying myself was the moment I was hooked. It had touched upon one of my desires, and if I had to choose one of the eight basic needs and wants *(Refer to Chapter 3: Why Do They Want to Do It?)*, my desire for that swing chair would fall under number five, "comfortable living conditions."

The question you need to ask yourself is: How many people know about my product? How many of them are aware that my product fulfills their needs and wants?

Identifying your customers' stages of awareness is the second step after identifying their desires.

And ... It's *not* just awareness about your product. It's also about ...

- What's available in the market?
- What does your competition offer?
- How many other products have they tried to fulfill that desire with in the past?

Eugene Schwartz also talked about <u>five stages of awareness</u> in his book, *Breakthrough Advertising.*[6] Once you identify where you stand in these stages, you will harness your message accordingly.

THE FIVE STAGES OF AWARENESS				
STAGE 1	STAGE 2	STAGE 3	STAGE 4	STAGE 5
The most aware	The customer knows of the product but doesn't yet want it	New products	Products that solve needs	Completely unaware market

The Five Stages of Awareness

Understanding your customers' awareness stage will help you communicate it back to them. Each stage requires a different approach. Just because something works for one stage doesn't mean it will work for another.

"Each of these stages is separated from the others by a psychological wall. On one side of that wall is indifference; on the other, intense interest." -Eugene Schwartz

1] Stage 1 – The most aware of your product

What does this mean?
Your customer is aware of your brand, your product, knows it can satisfy her desire, and wants it.

What can you do about it?
1. Name your product.
2. State a bargain price or discount, a free gift, free delivery, instant delivery, new store location, etc.
3. Tell them where to buy it.

Example:
Brand: IKEA

1. What's the product? All IKEA products
2. What's the bargain? Get 30% cashback when spending 500 DHS
3. Where to buy it? In-store or online

Source: https://www.facebook.com/ads/library/?id=1028775404562428

Stage 2 – The customer knows of the product but doesn't yet want it

What does this mean?

Your customer is aware of your brand and your product but doesn't believe it can satisfy her desire and doesn't want it because she:

1. Isn't aware of all it can offer her or doesn't know how it has improved.

2. Isn't convinced it could help her.

What can you do about it?

- Name the desire that will be fulfilled with your product.
- Crystalize the solution where she can imagine how the product satisfies her desire.

- Prove that the solution can be accomplished.
- Introduce a new mechanism of how the solution will be accomplished with your product as compared to your previous products or competition. ***Most important***

Now, let's look at examples of this concept being used in some real-life ads:

Example 1:
Brand: Hoover
Copy: "Hoover's new invention washes floors and vacuums up the scrub water."

Example 2:
Brand: Lewyt
Copy: "You breathe no dusty odors when you do it with Lewyt."

Based on these examples, start to think about how you would write eye-catching copy for an ad for the company Blu using the following criteria:

- *What's the desire?* Restore your hair to its natural beauty, leaving it soft and shiny.
- *What's the solution?* Filter your shower water as "unfiltered shower water can strip away your natural oils and leave your hair dry, frizzy, with split ends and can even accelerate hair loss."
- *What's the proof?* Social proof with a lot of testimonials such as – "I've been using it nonstop, and I love the results. Highly recommended, honestly."
- *What's the new mechanism?* The Blu Ionic Shower Filter.

- *What's the bargain?* [Bonus] 30% off.

Now, check what you came up with and compare it to what was actually used:

Source: https://www.facebook.com/ads/library/?id=901584434047822

"Price means nothing to a person who does not know your product, or want your product." -Eugene Schwartz

Stage 3 – New products: Your customer is not aware of your product but is aware of the desire and wants to satisfy it

What does this mean?

Your customer is not aware of your product but is aware of the desire and wants to satisfy it.

What can you do about it?
- Name the desire that will be fulfilled with your product.
- Crystalize the solution where she can imagine how the product satisfies her desire.
- Prove that the solution can be accomplished. *Most important*
- Show the mechanism of how the solution will be accomplished in your product.

Example 1:
- **Brand:** Dyson
- *What's the desire?* Cooled purified virus-free airflow at home.
- *What's the solution?* Dyson's purifiers.
- *What's the proof?* Not there.
- *What's the new mechanism?* Technology that detects and destroys unseen formaldehyde.

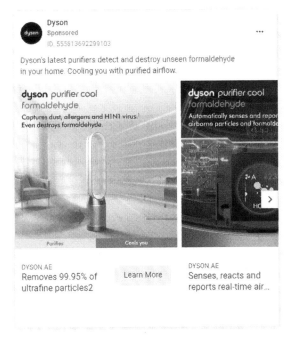

Source: https://www.facebook.com/ads/library/?id=555813692299103

Example 2:

- **Brand:** Alex Cattoni & The Copy Posse
- *What's the desire?*
  - IGNITE your business with crazy good copy.
  - Write a high-converting sales page.
- *What's the solution?* 5-Day Write & Ignite Challenge.
- *What's the proof?* Over the last decade, I've helped dozens of entrepreneurs and brands ignite their businesses with words that sell.
- *What's the new mechanism?*
  - Simple and proven 16-step formula.
  - Learn the exact steps to writing a high-converting sales page in 5 days.

- In this step-by-step video program, I will teach you the EXACT sales page formula and writing process I've used to help dozens of businesses execute iconic launches and campaigns.

Source: https://www.facebook.com/ads/library/?id=254333006282805

"The name of your product means nothing to a person who has never seen it before and may actually damage your ad if you have had a bad model the year before, or if it is now associated with the antiquated, the unfashionable, or the unpleasant." -Eugene Schwartz

Stage 4 – Products That Solve Needs: Your customer is not aware of the desire itself, but is generally concerned with a problem

What does this mean?

Your customer is not aware of the desire itself but is generally concerned with a problem. She needs to solve a problem but isn't aware that it can be fulfilled with your product.

What can you do about it?

- Name the need or problem.
- Dramatize the need so that the customer will realize how much she needs the solution.

Example 1:

- **Headline:** Do you make these mistakes in English?
- *What's the problem or need?* To write good English.
- *How is the need dramatized?* Refer to the mistakes she could be making in English.

Example 2:

- **Brand:** Hello Chef
- *What's the problem or need?* Easy home cooking.
- *How is the need dramatized?* Busy week, no time, stress

Source: https://www.facebook.com/ads/library/?id=600290701136143

Example 3:

- **Brand:** Moodfit
- *What's the problem or need?* Personalized home decoration.
- *How is the need dramatized?* Accessible home decoration tailored to your style and budget.

Source: https://www.facebook.com/ads/library/?id=193799842631288

Stage 5 - Completely Unaware Market

What does it mean?

Your customer is not concerned with the general problem. She is neither aware of a desire or a need (problem) and wouldn't admit it to herself.

What can you do about it?

- Do not mention price, product, function, special mechanism, or specific desire.
- Tell the customer what they are and make them self-identify. Then, concentrate on the state of mind of your customer at this moment, and echo an emotion, a dissatisfaction, an attitude that differentiates her from the crowd.
- Attract attention to get her to read the remaining content.

Example:

- **Brand:** Moodfit

- *How are they going to self-identify? Your style, Your home.* A quiz will also cater their results to their personalized taste.

- *How do you attract their attention to read the remaining content?* First, take our design quiz, "We'll let your style and our quiz do the talking."

- **Tip:** I would change "Take our design quiz" to "Take the quiz" to make it about the customer, not about the brand.

Source: https://www.facebook.com/ads/library/?id=519311349338408

3] Beliefs

Understanding your customers' past experience with similar products or with your competition will help you understand their stage of sophistication. For example, if I had tried a swing chair in the past and fell while swinging, I wouldn't be keen to get a new swing chair for my balcony. I wouldn't trust its quality because my past experience wasn't so great, especially since my previous retailer promised me the moon and couldn't deliver.

So, here you really want to understand your customers' beliefs. It's the beliefs that nudge that final decision to buy.

Once you understand your customers' sophistication stages and their previous experiences, you will be able to identify the correct methods that you can communicate to them to turn them from skeptics into believers and from novices into advocates.

The next section we're going to cover is the five stages of sophistication.[7] Once you identify where you stand in relation to these five stages, you will be able to harness your message accordingly.

THE FIVE STAGES OF SOPHISTICATION				
STAGE 1	STAGE 2	STAGE 3	STAGE 4	STAGE 5
You are the first in your market	You are the second in your market	You are the third in your market	You are in a competitive market, and the competition is introducing new mechanisms to achieve the same claim.	Your customer has heard it all and doesn't believe your or your competition.

The Five Stages of Sophistication

Stage 1 - You are the first in your market

What does this mean?

Your customer doesn't know about your product and hasn't received any information about it before. Once your customer becomes interested, they will become more enthusiastic about your product.

What can you do about it?
- Be simple and direct
- Name the need or the claim
- Dramatize the claim
- Introduce your product and prove it works

Example:
- Stage 1:"LOSE WEIGHT NOW!"

325

Stage 2 - You are the second in your market

What does it mean?

Your customer knows the product, and your competition has already educated her on the information she needs to know. Nevertheless, she is interested, so to grab her attention, you need to claim something far more dramatic than that of your competition, the first in the market.

What can you do about it?
- Copy the successful claim (of the first in the market).
- Dramatize the claim and drive it to the absolute limit.

Examples:
- Stage 1:
  - "LOSE WEIGHT NOW!"
- Stage 2:
  - "LOSE UP TO 35 POUNDS IN 3 WEEKS OR RECEIVE $50 OFF YOUR NEXT MEAL PLAN!"
  - "I AM 70 POUNDS LIGHTER, BUT SOMEHOW, I'M ALWAYS FULL AND SATISFIED!"

Stage 3 - You are the third in your market

What does it mean?

Your customer has heard it all: the claims, the exaggerations, and the extremes. She's so used to it that she's numb to it all. She feels nothing. Perhaps she tried a product or two from your competition, and she was faced with nothing but disappointment.

What can you do about it?
- Do not repeat or exaggerate claims.
- Introduce a new mechanism for solving the problem.
- Shift the messaging from WHAT the product does to HOW it works.
- Highlight performance, not accomplishment.

Example:
- Stage 1:
  - "LOSE WEIGHT NOW!"
- Stage 2:
  - "LOSE UP TO 35 POUNDS IN 3 WEEKS OR RECEIVE $50 OFF YOUR NEXT MEAL PLAN!"
  - "I AM 70 POUNDS LIGHTER, BUT SOMEHOW, I'M ALWAYS FULL AND SATISFIED!"
- Stage 3:
  - "CUTTING-EDGE FORMULA CLINICALLY PROVEN TO FLOAT FAT RIGHT OUT OF YOUR BODY!"
  - "FIRST EVER WONDER DRUG PROVEN FOR REDUCING ACTUAL BODY FAT!"

Stage 4 – You're in a competitive market, and the competition is introducing new mechanisms to achieve the same claim.

What does it mean?
Similar to Stage 2, your customer has already been introduced to a new mechanism for solving her problem by your competition. The new mechanism is producing sales, so similar to Stage 2, you will exaggerate, but instead, by magnifying the performance of your mechanism rather than the claim.

What can you do about it?
- Copy the successful mechanism.
- Exaggerate the performance of the mechanism compared to your competition.
- Make it surer, quicker, easier.
- Solve more problems.
- Overcome old limitations.
- Introduce additional benefits.

Example:
- Stage 1:
  - "LOSE WEIGHT NOW!"
- Stage 2:
  - "LOSE UP TO 35 POUNDS IN 3 WEEKS OR RECEIVE $50 OFF YOUR NEXT MEAL PLAN!"
  - "I AM 70 POUNDS LIGHTER, BUT SOMEHOW, I'M ALWAYS FULL AND SATISFIED!"
- Stage 3:
  - "CUTTING-EDGE FORMULA CLINICALLY PROVEN TO FLOAT FAT RIGHT OUT OF YOUR BODY!"
  - "FIRST EVER WONDER DRUG PROVEN FOR REDUCING ACTUAL BODY FAT!"
- Stage 4:
  - "FIRST EVER, DIET-FREE, WEIGHT-REDUCING WONDER DRUG!"

Stage 5 – Your customer has heard it all and doesn't believe you or your competition.

What does this mean?
Similar to Stage 3, your customers have heard it all, the claims, the new mechanisms, the exaggerations, and the extremes. She is tired of your promises, no longer believes in your advertisements, and doesn't want to hear from you or about your product anymore. So, in a way, the 5th stage of sophistication corresponds to the 5th stage of awareness discussed above and is handled with a similar strategy.

What can you do about it?
- Bring your customer to the ad, not through desire but through self-identification.
- Tell her what she is.

Example:
"WHY WOMEN CRY IN THE SHOWER ALONE . . ."

Note: For more examples, information, in-depth insights about the five stages of sophistication, read the book *"Breakthrough Advertising"*[8] by Eugene Schwartz. Trust me; you will love it!

Your Headline Strategy: *How are you grabbing your customers' attention?*

There is no formula for creativity, and therefore, I cannot share any templates for you to follow that guarantee successful copy. I can, however, share a process with you that will ignite your creativity and lead you to write copy that speaks to the hearts and minds of your customers.

You have created this product. Now, you want your message to be shared with the whole world. You want your target customers to know about this brand-new product you've designed. So, communicate it to them.

The first step in that communication is getting their attention, whether through your website homepage, an advertisement, product page, sales page, a blog post, or even a video.

The first thing your customers read or hear that must grab their attention is the headline.

But that's not the only "job" of the headline. It should also:
- Be targeted to your customer segments to "select" who is going to read further.
- Communicate a message, such as a need, job, challenge, or your product.
- Draw your customers to read further, view your video, or listen to your podcast.

Your headline could have many jobs, and what you decide to do with each job depends on your customers' desire, awareness, and sophistication. Your headline could make your customer want your product more and help her see how it will satisfy her desire. Or it could even introduce new proof, details, or documentation of how well your product can satisfy her desires—maybe even a new way of doing things that she is not accustomed to.

But, if your potential customer hasn't heard of your product yet, the headline could announce it to her and maybe even make her completely forget about the competition by showing her that your product alone can fulfill her desire in ways she hadn't thought of before.

To write your headline, you need to identify **four things:**

1. The most **powerful desire** that can be applied to your product *(Refer to Chapter 2: Why Do They Want to Do It?)*
2. The **challenges** stopping your customer from fulfilling those desires *(Refer to Chapter 4: What Is Stopping Them?)*
3. Your customer's **stage of awareness** of this desire and how your product solves it.
4. Your customer's **stage of sophistication** and if they believe in it.

Your headline's job is to make your prospects stop and read not just the first sentence but the *second* one in your ad. And the job of your second sentence? To make them read the *third* sentence. And so on.

The Four Components to Identify Your Headline Strategy

1] The Most Powerful Desire

In Chapter 3 *(Why Do They Want to Do It?)*, we spoke about your customers' desires and why they want to do the job that they want to do. In Chapter 5 *(What Problem Are You Helping Them Solve?)*, we talked about how your product is going to satisfy that desire.

Your customers may have many desires, but you don't need to tackle all of them in your messaging. The ones you want to focus your attention on will be based on the three dimensions of desire *(Refer to Chapter 3: Why Do They Want to Do It?)*:

- **Urgency, intensity, degree of demand to be satisfied.**
- **Staying power, degree of repetition, inability to be satisfied.**
- **Scope, the number of people who share this desire.**

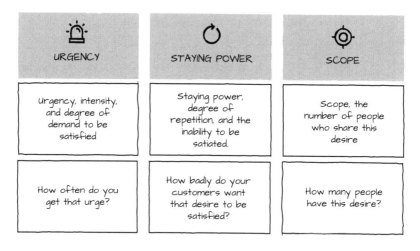

The Three Dimensions of Desire

As part of Chapter 5 (What Problem Are You Helping Them Solve?), you should have identified which customer desires you are tackling with your product.

Now, list all your customer desires based on the segments identified in Chapter 3 *(Why Do They Want to Do It?)* and measure them against those three dimensions. Choose a winner and then go to the next step, **your customer levels of awareness.**

2] Your Customer Challenges

Continuously research and ask your customers about their challenges. That's the best way to help them. Try not to assume anything even if you are experienced in your market.

In Chapter 4 (*What Is Stopping Them?*), we spoke about how to find out your customer's challenges, and I mentioned one of my favorite methods by Ryan Levesque, which is to ask what he calls the Single Most Important Question (SMIQ) that will lead you to uncover customer challenges.

SMIQ: "So, when it comes to X, what is your single biggest challenge or frustration right now? Please be as detailed and specific as possible."

You can then segment your customers based on their challenges, which will help you in your headline and copy strategy. When you speak to your customers, you will talk to them through their challenges, not their demographics.

And remember, you could always do some social stalking if you don't have access to customers. After all, social media is a blessing to those who take the time to use it to their advantage.

3] Your Customer Levels of Awareness

Identify your customer awareness level. Which of the following stages is your customer's awareness right now?
- **Stage 1 – The most aware of your product.**
- **Stage 2 – The customer knows of the product but doesn't yet want it.**
- **Stage 3 – New products: Your customer is not aware of your product but is aware of the desire and wants to satisfy it.**
- **Stage 4 – Products that solve needs: your customer is not aware of the desire itself but is generally concerned with a problem.**
- **Stage 5 – Completely unaware market.**

4] Your Customer Level of Sophistication

Next, identify the sophistication stage of your customers.
- **Stage 1 – You are the first in your market.**
- **Stage 2 – You are the second in your market.**
- **Stage 3 – You are the third in your market.**
- **Stage 4 – You're in a competitive market, and the competition is introducing new mechanisms to achieve the same claim.**
- **Stage 5 – Your customer has heard it all and doesn't believe you or your competition.**

Your Headline Strategy

Settle on your headline strategy to grab your customers' attention using their desires and challenges. Then, based on the awareness and sophistication stages of your customers, make sure to write the headline with the following strategies in mind:

At what stage is your customer's awareness about your brand, your product, and their desire and need?

Customer awareness stage	What does it mean?	What can you do about it?	Focus
Stage 1 - The Most Aware of Your Product	Your customer knows nothing about your product. Once they become interested, they will become more enthusiastic about your product.	• Name your product. • State a bargain price or discount, a free gift, free delivery, instant delivery, new store location, etc. • Tell them where to buy it.	• The product • The bargained deal
Stage 2 - The Customer Knows of the Product But Doesn't Yet Want It	Your customer knows the product, and your competition has already educated her on the information she needs to know. Nevertheless, she is interested, and so to grab her attention, you need to claim an even more dramatic claim than that of your competition, the first in the market.	• Name the desire that will be fulfilled with your product. • Crystalize the solution where she can imagine how the product satisfies her desire. • Prove that the solution is workable.	• The desire • The solution • The proof • The new mechanism - The most important*

Customer awareness stage	What does it mean?	What can you do about it?	Focus
Stage 2 - The Customer Knows of the Product But Doesn't Yet Want It (continued)		• Introduce a new mechanism of how the solution will be accomplished with your product compared to your previous products or competition. [Most important]	
Stage 3 - New Products: Your customer is not aware of your product but is aware of the desire and wants to satisfy it.	Your customer has heard it all, the claims, the exaggerations, and the extremes. She got used to it, and so it numbs her. She feels nothing. Perhaps she tried a product or two from your competition, and she was faced with nothing but disappointment.	• Name the desire that will be fulfilled with your product. • Crystalize the solution where she can imagine how the product satisfies her desire. • Prove that the solution can be accomplished. [Most important] • Show the mechanism of how the solution will be accomplished in your product.	• The desire • The solution • The proof - The most important • The mechanism

Customer awareness stage	What does it mean?	What can you do about it?	Focus
Stage 4 - Products That Solve Needs: Your customer is not aware of the desire itself, but is generally concerned with a problem.	Similar to Stage 2, your customer has already been introduced to a new mechanism for solving her problem by your competition. The new mechanism is producing sales, and so similar to Stage 2, you will exaggerate, but instead, by magnifying the performance of your mechanism rather than of the claim.	• Name the need or problem. • Dramatize the need so that the customer will realize how much she needs the solution.	• The need or problem dramatized
Stage 5 - Completely Unaware Market	Similar to Stage 3, your customers have heard it all: the claims, the new mechanisms, the exaggerations, and the extremes. She is tired of your promises, no longer believes in your advertisements, and doesn't want to hear from you or about your product anymore. In a way, the 5th stage of sophistication corresponds to the 5th stage of awareness discussed above and is handled with a similar strategy.	• Do not mention price, product, function, special mechanism, or specific desire. • Tell them what they are, and make them self-identify. Then, concentrate on the state of mind of your customer at this moment. Echo an emotion, dissatisfaction, or an attitude that differentiates her from the crowd. • Attract her attention so that she reads the remaining content.	Getting the customer to self-identify

Where do you stand in the market? How sophisticated are your customers?

Market sophistication stage	What does it mean?	What can you do about it?	Focus
Stage 1 - You are the first in your market.	Your customer is aware of your brand and your product, and she knows it can satisfy her desire so she wants it.	• Be simple and direct. • Name the need or the claim. • Dramatize the claim. • Introduce your product and prove it works.	• The need or claim, dramatized • Your product
Stage 2 - You are the second in your market.	Your customer is aware of your brand and your product but doesn't believe it can satisfy her desire and doesn't want it because she: 1. Isn't aware of all it can offer her or doesn't know how it has improved. 2. Isn't convinced it could help her.	• Copy the successful claim (of the first in the market). • Dramatize the claim and drive it to the absolute limit.	• The need or claim dramatized to the absolute limit
Stage 3 - You are the third in your market.	Your customer is not aware of your product but is aware of the desire and wants to satisfy it.	• Do not repeat things and do not exaggerate claims. • Introduce a new mechanism for solving the problem. • Shift the messaging from WHAT the product does to HOW it works. • Highlight performance, not accomplishment.	• A new mechanism • Performance

Market sophistication stage	What does it mean?	What can you do about it?	Focus
Stage 4 - You're in a competitive market, and the competition is introducing new mechanisms to achieve the same claim.	Your customer is not aware of the desire itself but is generally concerned with a problem. She needs to solve a problem but isn't aware that it can be fulfilled with your product.	• Copy the successful mechanism. • Exaggerate the performance of the mechanism compared to your competition. • Make it surer, quicker, easier. • Solve more problems. • Overcome old limitations. • Introduce additional benefits.	• The successful mechanism • Exaggerated performance • Additional benefits
Stage 5 - Your customer has heard it all and doesn't believe you or your competition.	Your customer is not concerned with the general problem. She is neither aware of a desire or a need (problem) and wouldn't admit it to herself.	• Bring your customer to the ad, not through desire but through self-identification. • Tell her what she is.	• Getting the customer to self-identify

Now you have your headline strategy.

Here is the thing. Remember, the one job your headline should do is to grab your customer's attention to read your copy, to read the next sentence, and the next sentence—until they choose to click "Buy Now!"

Your Copy Strategy: *How are you building up your customer's interest to buy?*

Once you've grabbed your customer's attention, now you have to keep it until they believe what you say and happily buy your product or service.

There are three dimensions of thought and feeling that you should tap into to strengthen your copy:[9]

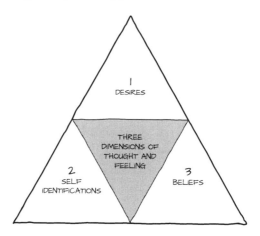

1. **Desires** – Sharpen your customer's desire. Make her see the fulfillment. Describe it well enough for her to see it, touch it, feel it, talk about it, and live it.

2. **Self-identifications** – This is what she sees herself as, her roles, or what she would envision her "perfect" self to be like. It's her personality, what she wants to be known for, and how your product will help her stand out from the crowd.

3. **Beliefs** – Speaking from the perspective of her opinions and beliefs, even if it's not what you believe, will grab her attention.

Build from that base and then prove how your product will satisfy her desires.

There are multiple ways to strengthen your copy with the above three dimensions in mind.

1] Intensification: Sharpen the desire, which is where curiosity begins. Strengthen it to become a genuine want and desire. A vague desire will manifest into a concrete image in your customer's mind once they understand exactly how your product will help them down to the smallest detail, including:

- What it is.
- How it works.
- What the benefits are over time—not just the immediate gratification.
- Who else has used it.
- If experts approve it.
- How it compares with the competition.
- How her life would be without it, and how it will help her avoid that pain.
- How easy it is to get the benefits of it.
- If it is guaranteed.

2] Self-identification: Your customer sees herself a certain way. She values her personality and role. Show how your product will help her play her role better and help others see her the way she wants to be seen. Her role is categorized as either a character role or achievement role. A character role can be described as brilliant, charming, radiant, or informed. An achievement role pertains to status, such as a father, homeowner, or executive.

3] Gradualization: If the benefits you are claiming as part of your product are a bit hard to believe, then start with what your customers believe in. Make them self-identify and say, "Yes, yes, that's me." Then, gradually show them how their beliefs are false by using the language of logic and repeating different forms of proof, such as statistics and expert findings.

4] Redefinition: Remove the objections to your product by stating that your product is THIS rather than THAT. Show the benefits of your product and how it makes her life easier, every day, and in situations when she would least expect it. For example, if your product is expensive and the objection relates to price, redefine the standard and switch the comparison to some other, more expensive standard.

5] Mechanization: Show *how* your product works and how it's different from everyone else's. Then, describe it, and explain how it will satisfy her desire, even if she tried everything else and it failed her.

6] Concentration: Show what else is in the market and emphasize how it doesn't fulfill her needs. Then prove to her that your product will provide her with what she wants by showing the superiority of your product, your promise, and how your product beats the competition.

With the three dimensions of thought and feeling and the method you use to strengthen your copy, the copy that leads your customers to buy will have the following "jobs":

- Build her desire for your product.
- Make her feel comfortable and complemented by your product. Help her visualize your product as part of her life, the life she is building.
- Make her believe what you are saying.

Which strategy are you going to use to strengthen your copy?

Chapter Quiz

Congratulations on making it through the final chapter of this book! You should now know everything you need to know to create products and services your customers will love. Remember to check the Final Thoughts section at the end of this book for some additional tips, tools, and an exclusive invite to my Product Innovation Studio! But first ...

Ready to test your knowledge with one last chapter quiz?

True/False

1: All customer desires can be profitable to your business. (True/False)

2: When your customer is "aware" of your brand and your product and knows it can satisfy her desire, you can use the name of your product in your headline strategy. (True/False)

3: When you introduce a product and are the "first" in the market, you have to educate your customer and provide her with information about the product. (True/False)

Quiz Answer Key

Answer 1: False. Customer desires are measured against three dimensions: urgency, staying power, and scope. Only then will you be able to answer the customer's question, "Is it worth it for my business?" When communicating with your customer, use that desire as reasoning for why it's worth it for them specifically.

Answer 2: True. When the customer knows your brand, your product, and knows it can satisfy her desire, all she wants to know now is where she can buy it and if she can get a good deal when buying it, such as a discount, free delivery, or a free gift.

Answer 3: True. When you are "first" in your market, it is your duty to take the burden off of your customer and educate your customer on your product. It is, however, important to be simple, clear, and appeal to the customer's need directly. Then, introduce how your product helps and provide proof that it works.

Putting It All into Action

You have worked so hard to craft your product and do all the work in the previous chapters. So, now it's time to put it all into action and decide on your hook strategy so that you connect with your customers and let them know about your product.

Here's your checklist:

1. Identify your customers' strongest desires for your product.
2. Identify your customers' awareness stage for your product.
3. Identify your customers' sophistication stage for your product.
4. Decide on your headline strategy based on your customers' awareness and sophistication levels.
5. Decide on your copy strategy based on the three dimensions of thought and feeling (desire, identifications, and beliefs).

Together we've reached the end! Or have we?

Some of these concepts are very hard to master; I am so proud of you for making it through to Chapter 9. Now that you did, I highly recommend going back and reading previous chapters to refresh your memory as needed. If you haven't done the exercises (I'm certain some of you skimmed over them), I highly encourage you to buckle down and put it all into action. Clarity comes from engagement, and progress comes from doing the work.

Remember, creating products and services that customers love is an iterative process. You can't possibly have all the answers up front, and the way forward is always to listen to your customers.

For more information, please read the Final Words section of this book. You're just two pages away!

References

1. "Moodfit.com." Mood Fit, n.d. http://www.moodfit.com/.
2. Phil M. Jones. Exactly What to Say: The Magic Words for Influence and Impact. Vancouver, BC: Page Two Books, 2018.
3. Eugene Schwartz, and Edelston, Martin. "Breakthrough Advertising ." Breakthrough Advertising. Brian Kurtz, 2017. https://breakthroughadvertisingbook.com/.
4. Schwartz, "Breakthrough Advertising," 2017.
5. Schwartz, "Breakthrough Advertising," 2017.
6. Schwartz, "Breakthrough Advertising," 2017.
7. Bobby Hewitt. "Eugene Schwartz Breakthrough Advertising Buying Stages." LinkedIn. LinkedIn, August 12, 2018. https://www.linkedin.com/pulse/eugene-schwartz-breakthrough-advertising-buying-stages-bobby-hewitt/.
8. Schwartz, "Breakthrough Advertising," 2017.
9. Schwartz, "Breakthrough Advertising," 2017.

FINAL
WORDS

Thank you for taking the time to read this book.

I hope it helped a few light bulbs go off in your head and opened your mind to new possibilities.

I wrote this book because I wanted to share with you what I learned the hard way. I want you to create products and services that your customers will fall in love with. More importantly, I want you to actually sell your products! Otherwise, what's the point, right?

I dive deep into this subject because I want customers to find value in what they are buying. I want them to find what they are looking for. By providing a product or service, you are making your customers' lives a little easier.

If you follow through with the entire process laid out in this book, right away you will be able to pinpoint the gaps that kept your customers from buying your product. More importantly, you will be equipped with the tools that will enable you to fix the situation and turn it around. You won't run out of ideas to help your customers. You will be able to go above and beyond and create products that your customers have never even thought of before. You will give them what they really need, despite the fact that they might not have explicitly asked for it, and have them thank you for it as if you were reading their minds.

I know you want to create amazing and unique products, and sometimes we get in our own way, thinking, *Ughhh ... This will take time, and I don't want to do it.* I encourage you to quiet this thought. The work you do will provide you with a goldmine of resources that will not only help you hone and craft your product to make it even better but can also be used for your branding, marketing, and copywriting strategies.

Take the "What's Your Product Design Personality?" Quiz if you haven't already. It's time that you truly understand your strengths and know which areas you should focus on. Please visit the following link to take the free quiz: https://www.sherwette.com/quiz.

Feel free to write me whenever you create or tweak a product. I want to know how you are doing and how your sales have changed since you started applying the methods mentioned in this book. Even if all you got was an "aha moment," I want to hear about it! What is one thing you learned while reading this book?

Email me at: me@sherwette.com. ☺

Here's to creating products that customers fall in love with!

The best way to move forward is to take one tiny step, then another step, then another one. Momentum gets you started, and then it gets you results.

What's the one thing that you will do today to create products and services customers love?

Hint: The "Putting It All into Action" sections have all the exercises that will get you started. ☺

Don't forget to tell me one thing you learned while reading this book! ☺

With lots of love,
Your consumer behavior gal ☺
–Sherwette

ACKNOWLEDGMENTS

I didn't know I was talented, let alone know I loved writing, until one day when my 7th grade English teacher, Mr. James, was reading my homework essay and asked me, *"Did you get this off the Internet?"* I was shocked and said, *"I didn't. I wrote it."* But then after writing a few essays, he got it. It was me, *definitely me.* And then I thought, *Huh, writing. I love writing.*

I never really entertained the idea of writing outside the homework assignments spectrum until I started my very first blog in 2010 and found that writing came so easily to me. I enjoy writing, especially when it comes to writing about topics I am passionate about, like consumer behavior. Back then, I had just graduated from university and my brother kept telling me to write a book. He said, *"Just do it."* I didn't think it was possible at the time. I thought, *Write a book? Really?* And since then, he never stopped encouraging me to *just do it.* And here I am, *Karim, just doing it.* ☺

Just doing it didn't happen in the literal form of just doing it. It took me years to come to the decision that I just had to do it and wait no more.

I am fortunate enough to have my family, my friends and coaches always supporting me to work on my passion and to *just do it*. Thanks, Mom, for your never-ending support to do my best in whatever I love doing.

Mohammed Abbas, you were my very first coach and my inspiration to take my passion seriously, and you use it to provide value and have an impact. Thanks for never giving up on me.

Cheers to Allison Tugwell; without her, this book wouldn't have come to life. It's because of her fun methods that I scribbled my very first mind map version for this book. And to Self-Publishing School, and specifically my coach, Kerk Murray, who provided me with the right guidance to get back on track after eight months of complete idleness to overcome my perfectionism paralysis and trust in the process.

Jeannie Culbertson and Sandra Wissinger: I am lucky to have worked with two amazing women. Thanks for your support, guidance, contribution and patience, I was able to write an even better book than I thought I would write.

Finally, special thanks to Yasmeen Safadi and Najeeb Jomaa, who constantly supported me emotionally and spiritually; thank you for always being there without even being asked. The past year was by far one my hardest years, and I wasn't going to get through it and finish writing my very first book without your support. It's what made this book happen.

AUTHOR
BIO

Sherwette is an author, writer, coach, and consultant based out of Dubai. Her area of expertise is business innovation and customer experience. Over the past 10+ years, she has brought world-class methodologies to large organizations in the Middle East to help them craft only the best customer experiences. She loves happy customers!

A self-proclaimed customer advocate, Sherwette voices the thoughts and opinions of the consumer, even in a room where they aren't present. Her curiosity keeps her open to always seeking new ideas and in turn, refining the old. Her favorite word is "why."

One of her mantras is "always learning" and "continuous improvement." She loves a day full of "aha moments." She is multi-passionate and loves to express her creativity in a variety of ways. Apart from writing, she loves reading books on psychology, painting abstract pieces, and cooking for her loved ones.

Sherwette is obsessed with consumer behavior and behavioral economics, and she loves to share her knowledge with others. She delights in seeing tangible results that build lasting relationships with customers. She shares tips on customer experience, service design, and product innovation in her blog, www.sherwette.com, and she can be reached at: me@sherwette.com.

You can also connect with her on:

- Twitter: https://twitter.com/sherwette
- Linkedin: https://www.linkedin.com/in/sherwette
- Instagram: https://www.instagram.com/sherwettesblog
- Facebook: https://www.facebook.com/sherwettesblog

THANK YOU FOR READING MY BOOK!

I hope you had a few "aha moments" while reading this book. ☺ Let me know what you thought of it! Leave me a review on Amazon or wherever else you purchased the book from. I would really appreciate your feedback. What did you learn from *Why No One Is Buying Your Product?*

Your opinion means so much to me! It will help make the next version of this book—and my future books—better.

If you learned something new from this book and felt that someone in your circle would benefit from it, please share a copy with them. ☺

Thank you so much!

With lots of love,
Your consumer behavior gal
—Sherwette

sherwette.com/bookreview

Made in the USA
Middletown, DE
20 December 2023

46483755R00212